A New Great Story

A New Great Story

Don Cupitt

POLEBRIDGE PRESS
Salem, Oregon

Cover and interior design by Robaire Ream
Cover illustration by Robaire Ream

Library of Congress Cataloging-in-Publication Data
Cupitt, Don.
  A new great story / Don Cupitt.
      p. cm.
  Includes bibliographical references (p.   ) and index.
  ISBN 978-1-59815-026-1 (alk. paper)
  1. Christianity--Psychology--History. 2. Church history--Psychology.
  3. Evolutionary psychology. 4. Philosophical theology. I. Title.
  BR110.C79 2010
  230.01--dc22
                          2010047118

If ever the search for a tranquil belief should end,
The future might stop emerging out of the past,
Out of what is full of us; yet the search
And the future emerging out of us seem to be one.

Wallace Stevens
Collected Poems (Faber), 2006 edn., p.129

TABLE OF CONTENTS

INTRODUCTION

I n this book I aim to set before the general reader a fully-modern alternative to the traditional "Grand Narrative" theology of Latin, or "Western," Christianity, commenting on it as I go along.

The old Grand Narrative was a huge Story of Everything that began and ended in eternity, running in between from God and his first creation of the angelic hierarchies, through the long history of man's fall and redemption, to the Last Judgement and the final triumph of the blessed. Its classic statement is to be found in *The City of God*, by St Augustine of Hippo (CE 354–430), the most important theologian of the early Western Church.[1] The great story occupies Books XI–XXII, and it dominated Western art until the late seventeenth century. English readers may have seen it very effectively dramatized in the open air, in the York Cycle of Mystery Plays. In something like strip-cartoon form it supplies the chief topics of mediaeval stained glass, and it is particularly well presented by the mosaics in St Mark's Cathedral, Venice. At the Reformation, all the principal protestant Reformers remained firm Augustinians. John Calvin, in particular, developed the old Grand Narrative theology with great rigour, aiming to convince the ordinary believer of God's absolute sovereignty over the whole of cosmic history, so that whatever might happen to him in the short run, if he had ever tasted divine Grace, he could be sure of his own final salvation. The traditions of protestantism that owe most to Calvin are variously called Reformed, Calvinist, Presbyterian, Puritan and also Independent, and Congregationalist. Today, the mantle of all those traditions has in effect fallen upon the (rather undenominational) Conservative Evangelical Protestantism that Americans and others have spread around much of the world in the last few generations.

The old-Western Grand Narrative theology is clearly not dead yet. It derives partly from ancient Zoroastrianism, and chiefly from the ancient Jews' national story as reported in the Hebrew Bible. St Paul began the work of modifying and expanding the Jewish narrative of the acts of God in their own history in order to turn it into a new Christian Great Story of cosmic fall and redemption (see Romans 5, 1 Corinthians 15, etc.). Another New Testament writer, the author of the letter To the Hebrews, tells his own more conservative version of the story, but he also manages to convey independently the classic Western sense of a great community's long march by faith through history, towards its promised future victory and glory. Today, the close alliance between American national sense of destiny and Israeli Zionism shows that the old Grand-Narrative, messianic-nationalist type of religious ideology still has some real political power, even though its former intellectual authority is now completely shot away.

The Latin Grand Narrative was indeed cosmic—but it was also geocentric. It started with the creation of the angels, described the revolt of Lucifer and his expulsion from Heaven, and then went on to relate how God had next created the visible universe and humankind in order to restock Heaven with human souls that had been road tested by their earthly life. But our first parents fell into sin, and in order to achieve his original aim God next launched the enormous project of first electing the Jewish people and then giving to them the Law of Moses. They fell too, and to save some humans God took the ultimate step of himself becoming incarnate as Man in Jesus Christ. The millennia of the Church would end with the return of Christ, and the establishment on earth of his millennial kingdom. Finally, after the last judgement God would at last get Heaven fully restocked and closed, while Satan and his cohorts, together with all the damned human souls, would be sealed up eternally in Hell. End of story.

This great story (or myth, *muthos* being the Greek word for story) provided the ideological basis—and the historical drive—of Christian civilization in the West. No very serious rival to it cropped up until the fourteenth-century Italian Renaissance, when people like Petrarch appear who seem to have simply stepped outside it. Petrarch was a lay poet, a man of affairs and a scholar, who found all the cultural framework he needed in platonic philosophy and in "human letters"—that is, ancient Greek secular literature. But because Plato remained the chief philosophical influence upon *both* Italian humanism *and* Christian doctrine, there was still much common ground, and the Church did not yet feel threatened. On the contrary, painters, architects, poets, and their aristocratic patrons soon became accustomed to a strange mixture of pagan and Christian mythologies that survives to this day. In the art gallery we are not in the least shocked or surprised to see Sandro Botticelli presenting us in one canvas with a delectable nude Venus, and then in another canvas with a Virgin Mother of God chastely dressed like a nun. It is simply a fact that the Italian Renaissance has left us all bilingual. Even the Renaissance Popes were bilingual, and the puritan poet John Milton does not hesitate to deck out his *Ode on the Morning of Christ's Nativity* with pagan figures.

As we have remarked already, the old Augustinian Grand Narrative theology was not seriously affected even by the Reformation. The leading protestants simply went on taking it for granted. But matters were very different in the seventeenth century, for now the rise of mathematical physics between Galileo and Newton radically changed the West's basic world-picture, and broke the old power of the Church. After the mechanization of Europe's world picture, people came to understand that all events in the physical Universe could be explained purely immanently in terms of matter, local motion and mathematical laws of motion. There was no longer any real room left for a Providence that guided all world-events towards the fulfilment of a single moral design, nor indeed for human freedom of action, nor for *any* supernatural beings or forces. There was nowhere to put the dead, because there was no space any longer either for the old Heaven above or for the old Hell beneath us.

Newton's triumph convinced the world that something extraordinary had happened. Human beings had found for themselves a new way to knowledge of unprecedented power and promise. Inevitably, attention began to focus upon questions of *method*, upon the human *mind* as a builder of knowledge, and upon the critique of *tradition*. In the past, most or all societies had been tradition-directed, but now the whole of Tradition needed to be rigorously examined, and (mostly) discarded. All this became the task of the Enlightenment.

The young David Hume's big (and very bright) work of philosophy shows in its full title the way the wind was blowing: *A Treatise of Human Nature: Being an Attempt to introduce the experimental* (= scientific) *Method of Reasoning into Moral Subjects* (= the humanities), 1739.[2] The new critical, questioning, head-on, human-centred method was applied in three volumes to human knowledge, to psychology and to ethics. Everything would be rebuilt: a new progressive, humanitarian, secular, science-based and fully-enlightened outlook would prevail everywhere.

Hume was broadly correct. The old ways of thinking, summed up as "Plato, Aristotle and Grand-Narrative theology," or simply "Augustine," had still just about held, only seventy years before, in the world of Milton, Bunyan, and the English Book of Common Prayer. Now, everything had changed. A new world beckoned.

Or so it seemed. In fact, the West found it extremely painful to relinquish its old faith, and extremely difficult to state its new faith with full philosophical clarity. Even yet, we have still not been able to settle into a lucid, confident and paradox-free secular-humanist world-view. What has happened is that in the double effort, to root out unjustified leftover metaphysical assumptions, and to avoid paradoxes of self-reflexivity, we have slipped further and further into scepticism—and in these respects Hume himself is still as instructive to read as almost any other modern philosopher.

The young Nietzsche's reaction to Darwinism is a good example. Being what he was, Nietzsche at once saw the paradox of self-reflexivity. If Darwin is right, then all our cognitive abilities are just survival-skills that we developed to help ourselves to get around, find food, pull a mate, and rear our young. In which case, we cannot distinguish between "real" truths and biologically-useful fictions. We cannot go beyond pragmatism: as Nietzsche puts it with deliberate coarseness, all our truths are illusions without which we cannot live. All our knowledge is practical or "applied," and none is "pure." What then about Darwinism *itself*? If we believe it, it may encourage us to set about conserving wildlife. It may teach us to love the earth, the body, the senses, and our own life while we have it. It has certainly proved a very illuminating, productive and even *healthy* theory to hold. There are then many ways in which Darwinism is a good and *useful* theory, and a way of thinking that soon becomes deeply interwoven with our whole vision of the world and of ourselves. But *objective truth*?— No, the theory itself seems to require us to give up that idea. But what then is Professor Richard Dawkins going to make of this conclusion? He's going to be cross as hell, and I sympathize. But how can he escape it?

At this point we remember that the old, Plato-Aristotle-and-Augustine world view had a big advantage. *It explained its own possibility*, by specially privileging human rationality. God was Reason itself, and had made a rationally-ordered created world. He had made us in his own image: he had made the rational, immortal human soul to be a finite counterpart of his own Infinite Reason. We were therefore specially *designed* to be able to track the order of the world and even to know our own Maker. The creationist theory is therefore smarter than it looks, because it explains its own possibility. Realizing the advantage this gave him, the Pope in the Encyclical *Humani Generis* (1950) cleverly handed the human body over to the Darwinists, but reserved the human rational soul for God. Thus the official Roman Catholic position remains to this day "creationist" about human rationality, and so avoids the nasty paradoxes that tend to arise all over the place when the scientific method is applied by us to ourselves. When science triumphs, it demolishes our grand pretensions, it shows that we are just clever animals—and thereby it undermines *itself*, too. And the greater the triumph, the greater the self-undermining. Got that?

This discussion has been intended to introduce a series of theses. *First*, once the scientific revolution had become securely launched, the traditional Grand-Narrative Christian theology was doomed. Neither at the individual level nor at the cosmic level is all of our life the acting out of a "meaningful" carefully-scripted Great Story with a guaranteed happy ending. Stories of *cosmic* Fall and Redemption have been displaced by the new cosmic history provided by natural science, and there is not the faintest chance that we will ever succeed in combining bits of the old supernaturalism with the scientific world-view. Psychologists are not going to start including spirit-possession amongst the various psychological states that they recognize, and meteorologists are not going to start weighing the number of prayers for rain currently being offered when they are drawing up their weather forecasts. Science contaminated with a bit of supernaturalism would no longer be real science. At present, we in the churches are living in denial, hoping that something will turn up to get us out of our difficulties. No: that is not going to happen. When we add in the extent to which the academic subject called "Theology" (biblical criticism, the history of Christian doctrine, the study of religions, etc.) has by now completely demythologized *itself*, then it is scarcely surprising that the old mainstream churches are today going rather crazy and fast collapsing. Every theologically-educated Christian is a closet sceptic. They all know it's not actually true anymore; at least, not in the old sense, but unfortunately they cannot say so. Not if they are Bishops, they can't.

The old religion is dead. In retrospect, it now seems very quaint and primitive. But it did in its heyday have certain intellectual and imaginative strengths and beauties, and it remains worth taking the trouble to find out exactly why it seemed for so long to so many very able people to be simply true. Till about 1850, an educated lay British person could still think that it was all just true: but then the great Victorian "crisis of faith" shows a whole generation of intellectuals like George Eliot, Matthew Arnold, John Ruskin and others realizing that the game was up.

Secondly, the Enlightenment idea of simply replacing Christianity with an uncomplicated science-based secular humanism that would invoke no more than a few universal ideas about reason, fact, experience, consciousness, human nature and the like—*that* project has turned out to be a failure. It is a dream whose pursuit has become a nightmare.

Thirdly then, I argue that there is a need now for a new Grand Narrative theology that will get us out of the nightmare. In previous writings I have given some intimations of it, and here I attempt a somewhat fuller statement, offering a new narrative that is fully secular and up-to-date in science and philosophy, but which avoids paradox and is religious.

The new task is not to spin a new updated *cosmic* history. As we shall see, it is the task of explaining the history of our "ideal culture." The main respect in which a human being differs from an animal is that the human being carries around in his or her head a whole world of cultural ideas *by* which he or she lives. We don't live in simple, unreflective and immediate contact with wild nature, responding to stimuli and seeking food, as animals do. We have this strange guidance-system in our heads, sharing it with other people in our own ethnic group. In the past, it was everywhere (broadly) religious, and was passed down from one generation to the next by tradition. Today, it has been changing so much and so fast that we find ourselves wondering how it first began, how it worked, and what has been happening to it in the modern period. Thus our new Grand Narrative will be a secular story about the whole process by which we have come to be what we now are. It will try to show how the world in our heads, the programming that I've called our "ideal culture," is made up of linguistic usages, myths, deep cultural assumptions, Gods, spirits, saints, our parents and our mentors, commandments, prohibitions and valuations. This great body of material has been slowly developed over many millennia. It has always been the framer, both of the only world there is, namely *our* world, and of ourselves too. We are *homines religiosi,* animals who've been made humans-in-a-world by the guidance-system in our heads. For most of our history it was indeed predominantly religious, and it guided our progressive development. But then around the time of the condemnation of Galileo everything began to change, eventually leaving us with the questions: "Why was it that for so long, in order to live, we had to *live by* a large body of religious ideas? And how are we to understand the queer fact that in the modern period religion seems to have led us beyond itself and become redundant"? In short, I want a Christian narrative, and a story that makes religious sense, about the birth, the life, the death, *and* the afterlife of God.

As we shall see, the new story is not a story of Fall and Redemption, but the strangely-roundabout story of how we have become ourselves. It starts in the violent chaos of animal experience. Language irrupts, lighting up the chaos and beginning to make things intelligible, and to shape life. The history of religion then develops as the story of how through language a world can be built, its law laid down, values posited, and long-term plans of action devised and carried out. Everything is first worked out at the supernatural level: the gods pioneered everything for us. Eventually, the fully developed Bronze-Age religious system produces a new breed of "enlightened" individual critics—prophets, philosophers—who criticize it all and bring it all back down into the human beings for whose sake the whole process has been going on. The Grand Narrative then culminates in the Galilean preaching of Jesus, and the launch of a new divine-human way of living. The whole story is then surprisingly repeated in the history of Christianity, which *also* goes out into mediaeval elaboration, and then through its criticism in the Reformation and the Enlightenment gradually returns into the individual modern human being who at last feels able to accept contingency and to build a life of love without any remaining fear or bitterness.

The new great story then describes a circular movement of objectification and return, which is then followed by a repeat or after-echo within the history of Christianity (and also some other world religions). It is all set out in tabular form on page 74f., below, if you want to jump ahead. But these ideas are largely new and quite difficult, so give yourself time to absorb them. I'm looking for a fully-developed theology for the age of modern physics, and inevitably it is very different from traditional forms of faith. Notice, too, that the two great processes, that by which the religious system is built up, and that by which it is broken down, are *equally* important to the whole story.

Cambridge 2010
Don Cupitt

1

THE USES OF "GOD"

To avoid misunderstanding of the story that follows, we need a few preliminary remarks about the very over-stretched and irritating word "God."

In contemporary English there is a common use of "God" as a convenient synonym for religion in general. The "god-slot" is the period each Sunday evening in Britain during which the principal television channels are, or were, required to broadcast material that is broadly religious. A recent notoriously loyal and combative Prime Minister's Press Secretary famously snapped at a journalist: "We don't do God," meaning that no politician managed by him would ever be allowed to become involved in religious controversy. In much the same spirit, I will need in my new grand narrative to make some use of the word "God" in a wide sense, especially at the beginning. It will signify the whole supernatural world—at first, a world of archetypal, mythic animals and other beings, then a world chiefly of spirits, then a polytheistic world of gods under the presidency of a Sky-Father, and only then finally the One capital-G God of "Abrahamic monotheism," in the common tradition of Jews, Christians and Muslims. Thus the word "God" at first signifies a complex scrimmage of invisible, obscure beings and powers, and only over several millennia does it become more systematized, centred, and unified, until it culminates in the One God.

Cosmology and psychology developed along similar lines, but were usually a little later. Only gradually, as people settle down in one place, does the world become centred around an *axis mundi*, law-governed and unified. The process has been finally completed only in modern times, and something similar may be said of the self, which began and long remained plural. Even today one often hears phrases like "Body, mind and spirit," which indicate that the human self is not yet fully centred and unified.

There seems, then, to be a *prima facie* case for holding that theology was (and in some eyes still is) the queen of the sciences, in the sense that almost all, or perhaps simply *all* of our most basic ideas about the human self and the world were pioneered in connection with God.

For example, a major step in human development was the moment when our ancestors gave up being nomadic hunter-gatherers or pastoralists, and instead settled down and became farmers. This was a huge and enormously difficult step for nomads to take, eventually requiring quite new institutions: dominion, territory, law, land, property, inheritance, fixed stone houses, boundaries, money and marketing, and so on. How on earth did nomads ever persuade themselves to take such a leap into the unknown? They didn't yet have the language even to *discuss* the issues that were before them.

Nevertheless, they did it, because God led the way in a manner familiar to all readers of the Hebrew Bible. God announced through his spokespeople that he would not always be a nomad, marching at the head of his people and living in a tent. He intended to settle down. He had chosen a territory, and was promising it to his people as their inheritance. He would settle: instead of being a winged spirit continually on the move, he would sit still, grandly enthroned in a fixed stone House at the centre of a Holy City. From this seat of authority the Holy Land's entire life would be regulated . . . and so on. Thus it was *via* religious thought that nomads first imagined and were then prevailed upon to accept one of the greatest changes in all human history: *civilization* (from *civis*, a city).

This example immediately prompts us to think of many others. For example, nomads carry no *chairs* with them. God pioneered seating, insofar as the Ark was already a portable throne, and from God's throne all other top seats derive—the top seats of kings, of bishops, of judges and professors, of Presidents (Latin, "sitting first") and other Chairs and Chairpersons. Similarly, Bronze Age archaeology reminds us that the earliest settlements had been very untidy huddles. The formal straight *street* was first invented not for humans, but for the gods to use as a Processional Way, along which they were carried annually when they were taken out to be shown to the people.

There are endless further examples. *Curtains* are a good one. There is a relic of the earliest curtains, hanging between riddle-posts and screening the altar, in a church near you, for the first curtains shielded a god's holiness. (Remember the Temple veil?) Now, curtains protect your *privacy*. Modern human privacy and the right to it derives historically from the god's desire for privacy in his "sanctum," for every theological term, and every prerogative of God tends over the centuries to become democratized and secularized. In the same way, divine service in time became royal service, domestic service and public service.

Thus we get a first glimpse of one of the main theses of this book. We differ from other animals in that we relate ourselves to life with the help of, and we live by, a complex body of ideas, our "ideal culture," that we carry around in our heads. We drank it all in as we learnt our mother tongue, and grew up as fully-functioning members of our own society. Originally it consisted of much more than just tribal customs and ways of speaking: it was a complex religious ideology—because religion was originally a highly progressive force. Only religion had the *indirectness* and the

sheer *power* needed to drag lazy reluctant animals out into
the light of our modern language-lit human consciousness
of being-in-a-world. Only religion had the power to compel
nomads to settle down, and bind themselves to a territory,
to a political obedience, to property rights, to festivals and
markets and all the rest.

The principle that I have just sketched can now be extended to a much grander level. God, according to the most
familiar of all the mythologies that deal with the matter,
was the first conscious person, the first to see an ordered,
lit-up, unified world and to know that it was his. "All the
beasts of the field are mine / and the cattle upon a thousand
hills," he declares proudly.[3] Yes indeed. Religion was originally a highly progressive institution: it first invented, and
then gradually transferred to us, all our most basic ideas
about ourselves and our world. It dragged us out of Nature;
it made us human. That is the true and only sense in which
God created us. We are still made in his image.

In later religious thought God is often described as being *both* our Beginning *and* our End, our Alpha and Omega,
the Primal Ground as well as the Final Goal of our existence.
Looking back to our human origins, stories about God as
our "beginning" may have the function of helping us to see
the peculiar centrality and authority of the religious realm.
It made us what we are. Looking in the opposite direction,
namely forwards, we see that the idea of God continually
requires us to criticize and to set aside old ways of doing
things, and old ways of constructing the world and the self,
and move forward into new and higher levels of consciousness, freedom, and Emptiness. The old ways always seem
more solid, and leaving them behind always seems like a
loss of faith and a movement into darkness and emptiness.
So it is always part of orthodox doctrine that God is *incom-
prehensible*: featureless, dark and Empty. Getting closer to
God is getting freer and freer, more and more Emptied-out.

Broadly speaking, religion continued to be a progressive force in human affairs until the late sixteenth century. But with the rise of science, it was natural enough that the new scientific theories of the world should be measured up against and compared with the long-established religious doctrines that were seemingly in possession of the field. Galileo, in particular, is famous for having demolished Aristotle's natural philosophy, and for declaring that God was a mathematician and an engineer. Against this background, and especially in the English-speaking world a very large shift in the way people thought of God began to take place. The old metaphysical God, based chiefly upon the philosophy of Plato and later Platonists, had been the Form of the Good, a transcendent object of aspiration, mysterious, "beyond being" and dwelling in mystical darkness, ever since biblical times. Since the thirteenth century the classic old metaphysical theism had been somewhat modified by the incorporation of a good deal of Aristotle's metaphysics of Being and his philosophy of nature. But now, with the sudden huge influence of scientific theory, the old Plato-and-Aristotle philosophy of God declined rapidly. To replace it, a new and more scientific God was invented, the God of the Argument from Design. This new God was based on a figure in Plato's *Timaeus*, by him called the "Demiourgos." He was a finite world-architect, a mathematician and engineer. In the new mechanical universe the old ways to God (as formal cause or final cause of the world, etc.) were blocked off, but it seemed that you could still make out a case for the existence of God as an empirical hypothesis to explain why the world-machine was so elegantly designed—and, in particular, how living organisms could be such elegantly designed little machines, perfectly adapted to their mode of life.

In the English-speaking world, this rather novel philosophy of God quickly became very popular, being propagated assiduously by a long line of Royal-Society theologians between Newton and Darwin. It was a very shallow response to the intellectual needs of the time. Its limitations were pointed out, and it was firmly refuted, by Hume and Kant during the eighteenth century. Nevertheless, it was so easy and convenient that Evangelical Protestants cling to it to this day, in spite of Darwin's comprehensive refutation of it. Even yet, few people seem aware of the size of the gulf between the transcendent God of the old metaphysical theism and the finite Designer who shapes the world out of pre-existent matter.

In particular, God had become associated almost exclusively with *cosmogony*, quasi-scientific theorizing about the origin of the Universe in general, and living creatures (including Man) in particular. The side of religion which aspires after, and tries to work towards, the ideal *goal* of the religious life, was lost; and to this day the Evangelicals reject the application of critical thinking to religious ideas, and have no spirituality (or "ascetical theology") at all. And yet, amazingly, they manage to present themselves as "traditional Christian believers." In fact, their Christianity is as hollowed out and reduced as the "Buddhism" of the Hong Kong temples, and one can only applaud Professor Dawkins for his attack upon them.

In conclusion, the idea of God largely lost its old progressive drive during the period of the scientific revolution. Preoccupied with trying to defend a crudely "realistic" notion of God as an empirical hypothesis to account for the existence of the cosmos and the adaptation of living organisms to their environment, people largely lost touch with the traditional mystical theology. By the middle of the eighteenth century the old metaphysical theism was dead, anyway—at least in the English-speaking world.

All this helps to explain why the new Grand Narrative presented in this book is so very different from the traditional one. The new great story is more like Hegel's—but in a very English idiom. It will be a sort-of history of our ideal culture, showing how, within the development of religious thought, first God, and then the world, and then we ourselves were produced and developed. We (sort-of) made God, and God then gradually made us and our world what they are—and are still becoming—today.

2

THE USES OF "WORLD"

Given his unique literary status, it is not surprising that people should attempt to write biographies of William Shakespeare. But he lived in a period when most people's lives were only just beginning to be better documented: parish church registers, for example, first began to be kept from around the year of his birth. As a literary genre, biography scarcely yet existed. So it comes about that modern would-be biographers are faced with the task of constructing a loaf out of the very few crumbs of personal information about Shakespeare that have survived.

How are they to do it? Mainly, by building up a detailed picture of Shakespeare's *age*, his *times*, his *milieu*, his setting-in-life (*Sitz-im-Leben*) — in short, his *world*. "World" is an old Germanic compound meaning a man's age: "w(e)oruld," related to the Dutch *wereld* and the German *Welt*. We are all of us deeply interwoven with our worlds, so the idea is that if we put together the few scraps of personal information about Shakespeare that have reached us, together with the evidence about his personality that may be gleaned from such writing as his sonnets and also a detailed knowledge of his "world," then we may be able to conjure up some sort of portrait of the man.

Thus the principal use of the term "world" in everyday language refers to the whole social and cultural setting within which a person lives: **the world and his wife** means "everyone." Often we use the word in a sense which implies that one should *not* allow society completely to govern all one's thinking and dictate one's values, as **a man of the world** does. Those who do that may **go up in the world**, but it's not a good thing to be so **worldly**. Nevertheless the fact remains that we are all of us period pieces, shaped by, as well as helping to shape, the times in which we live.

A corollary of this discussion is the recognition that for there to be a world at all, there has to be at least one person, and usually a whole society of people, whose world it is. There are no ownerless worlds. A world is projected out or built up around itself by a human subject, or an organism, and becomes a personal den, a territory, a drawing-room, a workshop, a kitchen, a study, a *lair*. Human beings in particular are so sociable and communicative that a large human group—a whole society—builds up in time a very large and highly-differentiated common world, structured and lit up by their language.

It seems that only we humans have a world in this last and strongest sense. But the situation has undoubtedly changed since the modern study of animal behaviour got under way a lifetime ago with the work of figures such as von Frisch, Köhler, Lorenz, Lack and Tinbergen. It seems that many animals can and do have territoriality, social structure, communication-systems, "cultural" transmission of acquired skills, some degree of subjectivity, and so on. In which case we have to acknowledge that many an animal is beginning to be a-self-in-a-world. It now seems that Descartes was mistaken in drawing such a very sharp line between humans and animals as he did, and that Leibniz, who believed in continuity, was more nearly correct.

A few years ago I would have said that there remains a big difference, in that whereas we have theories about them, animals don't actually have theories about *us*. We look at them, wondering what it is for them to be themselves, and wondering whether they could ever possibly speculate about *us*. But it now appears to me that in some cases—dolphins, in particular—the barrier between two different species may be crossed imaginatively from *their* side as well as from *ours*. They may recognize an affinity between the two species, much as we do, and help a distressed, drowning human to the surface just as they help one of their own.

Thus it now seems that there is full continuity between animal and human life. Historically, the three great dimensions of our being—language, consciousness, world—have all evolved together and continuously out of our animal background, with no clear cut-off point at which our forebears stopped being animals and started being humans. But on general philosophical grounds we may still say that the human take-off into sustained growth happened at the point when language and consciousness and world, all of them developing in parallel and all of them coextensive, became continua with no gaps. There are no holes or gaps in language: in principle, it covers and deals with everything. There are no holes in consciousness, just as there are no holes in time or in the visual field; and similarly there are no holes in the natural world. When language and consciousness and world are fully continuous, then human beings have "come into" their own human world as one comes into an inheritance, and the take-off into history can occur. We don't know the date of this for sure, and perhaps never will, but I'd put it some time in the Upper Palaeolithic, with the full completion of the process being quite recent. (I provisionally opt for this very late dating because, as we now see, languages and cultures can evolve very fast.)

So far, I conclude that the primary world is simply the human world, and the new grand narrative that we have promised will try to tell the long, strange, roundabout story of the genesis and growth to adulthood of the modern human self in its human world. I have drawn an implied distinction between the world of everyday life, the human "lifeworld" which has to be somebody's world, and "the Universe" of natural science which does not; and this distinction is similar to the long-established distinctions between *saeculum* and *mundus* in Latin, and *aiōn* and *kosmos* in Greek.

With the huge prestige and the rapid growth of modern natural science, there has been a tendency in recent centuries to equate the world with the Universe of our current cosmological theory. People then start supposing that "the creation of the world by God" can be redescribed in modern terms as God's having caused the Big Bang to occur.

This is a very bad misunderstanding. Physics does not deal with human beings, and the world that it describes is a theoretical construct put together within, and projected out *from within* the ordinary human life-world, which remains prior. Experimental testing of theories always happens *within* our lifeworld. The Big Bang or "initial singularity" is a postulate, an ideal limit to which our physical theory points back. It is in principle *not* something that could have been *caused*, by God or anything else, and in principle *not* something that we or anyone else could have observed. So it was not, in our human-world sense, a "real event," and there is no sense in talking about or trying to think about something "prior to" the Big Bang, just as there is no sense in trying to continue travelling northwards after you have reached the North Pole.

Thus, as I have earlier suggested, when we talk about God's creation of the world we are not talking about the secondary theoretical construct that we call the Cosmos, the Universe, or (sometimes) "Nature." We are talking, instead, about God's production of human beings in full possession of their own human world—a very long process that probably took well over ten thousand years, and has only recently become complete. What we are talking about is the history of religious thought, for it was religion that gradually enabled human beings to become unified selves, able to look upon a stable, unified, lawgoverned world with approval and recognize it as their own, and as the theatre in which they live and act out their lives. As we have already suggested, God was the first person singular, the first to be able to say, "I am, and this is my world, within which I can project out and implement my planned course of action." Everything, but everything had to be imagined *via* God, and over the millennia everything that we originally ascribed to God was gradually transferred to and appropriated by ourselves. So, over a long period, God did create everything out of nothing, and made us everything that we have gradually become, even to the extent of himself eventually becoming fully human and dying into us.

The whole new grand narrative that we are going to imagine is therefore the story of how it was through God, or through religion, that over a very long period we gradually became ourselves and came into our inheritance, which is simply our life in this world as we can now live it. It was God who enabled us to imagine what we could become, and who gradually helped us to become it. In effect, we created God in order to be able through him to represent our own future growth to ourselves. God was one for us to aspire after.

3

IN THE BEGINNING

Shut your eyes. What do you see? In a slightly-unfo-cussed way (because your two eyes are no longer co-ordinating properly), you see a surging, foaming, flicker-ing tumult of minute specks of faint light against a dark background, specks so tiny that you wonder if each one may be connected with a single rod or cone on your retina. The whole field shimmers and twitches continuously. In front of it there seem to me to float patches of yellowish-green light—evidently after-images of the windowpanes that I was looking at when I closed my own eyes just now. Otherwise, the most-nearly intelligible events I can experi-ence are the sudden flashes when someone switches on a light, or shines a torch at my closed eyelids.

This is our quickest access to something like the Primal Chaos, the animal's experience of a world not yet lit-up, formed and stabilized by language, and screened in con-sciousness. Other senses offer something similar. Thus, behind our definite "formed" hearing of this or that there is always the faint hiss, crackle and spatter of what sound recordists call "atmos" and radio hams call "white noise." For the sense of hearing, the world *minus* language equals white noise. (Music being itself a forming of noise into in-telligible, beautiful sound. Music is already a language.) In the case of the so-called sense of touch, we have a faint and usually-overlooked general bodily awareness of very great

range and complexity. It includes sensations of temperature, of our own pulse and breathing, of the various degrees
of tension in our muscles, and of the whole skin-surface of
the body. Just at the moment, you have very complex sensations associated with every part of your face, including especially your mouth and throat, your eye-sockets and your
nasal membranes, your cheeks and your ears. We rarely
attend to all this, which is odd.

Now return briefly to the strange, glittering, turbulent
dark field of specks you were looking at with your eyelids
closed. This time, open your eyes and look equally intently
at the sky, or at a white-painted wall. Exactly the same
crowded screen of tiny twinkling spots is still there! It
hangs against a whitish background like a very thin veil of
gossamer: perhaps it is a curtain of sparkling elvish chain-
mail between you and the language-formed external real-.
ity of clouds and sky, or of wallpaper. With a little careful
attention we can learn to see that that sheer, gauzy mist of
primal chaos is ubiquitous: it hangs before our eyes all the
time, just as a faint susurration of "atmos" whispers in our
ears all the time.

Back to your closed eyes, and consider now how empty
of structure the dark speckled field is. It is finite and temporal, but time here is not linear: it is not "going anywhere" in
any consistent fashion, and nothing you see has any stable
shape or form, except perhaps those after-images. What
you now need to observe is the fact that this chaotic emptiness also empties out the self. It makes you nothing but
a bare point, a minimal observer. When the world (or the
Other) is Empty, the self is emptied out too. There can't be a
stable self until there is a stable, ordered world.

This meditation has been introduced to get you accustomed to the idea of chaos, a primal, original and pre-
conscious state of things. In modern physics there is no
absolute Void, because even at absolute zero (-273°C) there
is still a faint speckling and splattering of particles coming

into existence and slipping out of it again. There is no absolute Being and no absolute Nothingness: existence itself is merely a matter of probability. And this minimal fizz at absolute zero temperature is called "quantum foam." In a similar way I am suggesting that every sentient organism, every living thing with acutely-quivering sensory surfaces, always has just a little (but only a little) sentience and subjective life; and I am offering what you see when you shut your eyes as a natural image (or even example) of it. It's a ceaseless low-level flickering of the senses, no more. There's no language yet, no forming of things, no unified world, and no self.

If, in early Palaeolithic times, or perhaps much further back, that was once all we were and all we had, how did we ever manage to make any progress? How did we ever develop language, consciousness, a self, a world? As we noted, in addition to the continuously-foaming background, there are also occasional sharp and sudden flashes of sensation and feeling, most typically when something biologically-significant presents itself. The thing that presents itself may be a potential predator, or a rival, or a potential mate, or a threat to one's offspring, or an unexplained sudden noise or movement—and there are a few other possibilities. But when the organism is suddenly jolted into rigid stillness and attentiveness, it must very speedily *classify* the stimulus that has suddenly presented itself. It must get the classification right, so that it can produce the appropriate response as quickly as possible.

Here I must briefly introduce the biological term "stimulus generality." When an organism produces the appropriate response—reflex or trained—to a biologically-significant stimulus, we are not talking about a stimulus that must be *exactly* the same every time: we are talking about a certain *range* of possible presentations that are each adequate to provoke the same response. (Behaviourist psychology discovered this long ago.) Any one of a certain *range* of presentations can count as a case of being threatened by the feared predator; any one of a certain *range* of presentations can be taken by the organism to be a case of meeting a serious rival who needs to be fought; any one of a certain *range* of presentations will be taken by the organism to indicate the approach of a potential mate and will therefore trigger courtship-behaviour, as has often been remarked in the case of William Jefferson Clinton. And so on: we have enough to state a number of theses about the first origins of consciousness, language, knowledge and religion.

1. As simple and elementary a piece of behaviour as any other is a sentient organism's capacity to produce very quickly the appropriate response to a biologically-significant stimulus. But for this to work well, the organism needs to be able to *classify* any item from one range of particular presentations as the Predator-animal, or from another range as the Prey-animal, from another range as the Mate, the other sex of its own species in season, from another range as possible Danger, another as Threat to my Young, and so on, producing in each case the appropriate behavioural response without error. That is, the organism already uses the notion of a Universal Term, a common noun, a class name, the standard example, the Type or Kind, under which various particular presentations are very speedily seen to fall.

2. In short, the Universal is the standard, behaviour-guiding example of every kind of thing. It is very important. It comes *first*. It is the Sign. It makes the world intelligible, it guides life. It is essential for survival. Most early humans hunted or herded only one species of animal, or only a few species, and they had the strongest possible incentive to study that species, to observe it very closely, and to get to know its typical behaviour really well. And there were similar incentives to identify the few significant predators accurately, and to go through the reproductive cycle accurately, by correctly reading the relevant signs at each of the various stages in the cycle.

3. All this makes it entirely intelligible, from a biological point of view, that the earliest surviving works of art were representations of animals and of human women, and that the first religious objects were totems. The totem animal was the Universal Gazelle or Lion, the standard, normative, ancestral Founder and parent of its whole kind, and the whole system of totems was the first form of ideal culture: a simple roadmap of the environment that told you exactly what you must look out for, and how to react to it.[4] The totem animal was in due course to develop into the ancestral Mythic Being, the spirit, the angel, the god; and theriomorphic (animal-shaped) images of the divine survive to this day in relatively-archaic religions such as Christianity and Hinduism—the Lion, the Lamb, the Dove, the Serpent. Regiments and sporting clubs still have animal mascots.

4. How did the totem animal develop into a spirit? If we return to the primal Beginning, which we accessed simply by shutting our eyes, we can now see that although we seemed there to be confronted by almost pure chaos, it did offer two possible starting-points for human intellectual development. It allows us to open the distinction between something that moves and something that makes it move. Even Darwin's dog made that distinction, when it barked at an open parasol resting on the ground, which shifted in response to a tiny puff of wind. Every time we suddenly sense an unexpected motion in the environment but don't see any obvious reason for it, we still begin to flirt with animism, the belief in spirits. We *do*.

The second starting-point for later thought is one that is easily missed. When we looked at the inside of our eyelids, or when we lie on our backs and gaze up at the empty sky, the self seemed emptied-out till it became no more than a bare lookout or *Aussichtspunkt*. But there still *is* the fact of observation, and it does supply a glimmer of transcendence. Like the cameraman in cinema, it tends to be overlooked, but it is always there.

We thus find that God was originally born from three roots: the Totem or Universal term, the unseen mover or Animator, and the (obscurely-transcendent) Observer. It was a birth that took place for entirely-intelligible biological reasons, we humans being highly-sociable animals who hunt and are hunted, and who need some weaponry and very close collaboration in order to survive and to get our young raised. For the moment, file away the point: the totem-animal was the guiding Universal, the first god, and older than the self.

5. We can now envisage the form that the earliest religious rites may have taken. Men gather to prepare for the hunt: perhaps they are in or by a cave or other place where there are rock-paintings of the prey animal. A fire burns. The men are dressed and equipped for the hunt. The ritual is led by a shaman who specializes in leading the way into an altered state of consciousness, produced with the help of music or plant-materials. In this altered state of consciousness (equated with the emergent supernatural world), the men dance and bind themselves together into a common enterprise, focussed upon the prey animal, the animal around which the tribe's entire life revolves. To get everyone's mind focussed upon the prey animal, tokens of it such as its horns or its skin may be worn by the shaman, or by all.[5]

The point of all this ritual is clear enough. Living at subsistence level, early hunter-gatherers were very idle characters with a very short attention-span. The men were seriously tempted to lie back and let the women do all the work. It was ever thus, and it still is. It took considerable discipline and ritual to bind men together in a collective enterprise, the hunt, very strictly focussed upon the prey animal. The ritual presented the Prey to them in its most authoritative form: it was not just any old deer, it was The Gazelle, the specific kind that they must stay collectively-focussed-upon until the hunt had succeeded. It would have to be seen as a grave sin, a betrayal of one's own masculinity, to abandon one's comrades and return home empty-handed. A man must not give up. And so on: one sees here the very beginning of worship and of ideas of religious law, and of guilt and shame.

Even at this earliest stage of its development, religion evidently has several very important social functions, epistemological, social and ethical. It equips us with a very basic map of our world and the ability to identify its most salient features. It binds people together into a cohesive, powerful group that can co-operate effectively, and it supplies us with the very beginnings of an ethic—in the case I have cited, the still-powerful ethic of comradeship and the male bond—backed up with simple ideas of shame. Frankly, every man would rather die in the hunt than be thought by other men not to be a man. And all of this, very early religion does principally through art and ritual. Finally, we have glimpsed the very beginnings of belief in a supernatural world. It is accessed when chewing or sniffing some intoxicant leaves, or music, induces a state of light trance. In that state the shaman meets and communes with the totem animal in its sacred, spirit-form, and in that state ordinary men are more suggestible, and ready to be solemnly committed to some great common enterprise.

The story as I have told it has centred mainly upon men and the hunt, because cave art appears to tell just this story. We might instead have told a different and perhaps more Freudian story about kinship, about a Primal Father, and about our first parents.[6] But, interesting and attractive though the story about kinship and ancestors is, there is much less evidence of its antiquity.

What features of religious thought have not yet appeared? The most notable is that cosmology and psychology, the world and the self, are not yet "centred" and unified. Precisely *because* they were wandering hunter-gatherers, the earliest humans did not have a strongly-centred world, with an axis around which everything turns. Instead, they saw their environment as a somewhat-disorderly scrimmage of Powers, some of which were benevolent, some grandly indifferent, and some malevolent in their disposition towards us. Their world had only a few regularities and stable identities, and religion duly fastened upon them. But much was fearsome, fluid, undefined and subject to mysterious transformations.

Very notably, in the very early times we have been thinking about, the self was similarly vague and not-yet-centred. It was an empty theatre, and a variety of beings might enter it and pass across the stage. The gods, and, above all, *animal kinds*, had clearly-identifiable psychological traits, distinct personalities and names, long before *we* did! Thus the supernatural world is older than the world of the individual human self; and we attributed distinct personality-traits to lions and lambs, to dogs and cats, to hawks and doves, long *before* we learnt to attribute distinct personalities to ourselves. In fact, *most* human personality traits have been borrowed from prior animal models! The world of nomads is a world that hasn't yet settled down, and in those days we too hadn't yet *settled down* to become anything very definite.

4

SETTLING DOWN

M any Christian theologians, especially in the tradition of Calvin and Karl Barth, have wanted to claim that the Bible as a whole bears witness to just one systematic theology—their own, naturally. They were quite wrong. In fact, so conservative is religion that much or most of the entire history of religions can be found in the Hebrew Bible—including some startlingly-archaic ideas of God (coupled with indignant denials by God of his own past). Thus in Genesis alone there are relics of a time when God was plural (the title "Elohim," and "the Old Testament Trinity" who appear to Abraham), to be put beside the later insistence upon the divine Unity. There are veiled relics of the time when God was an animal totem ("the Bull of Jacob" alluded to in the title "the Mighty One of Jacob," Genesis 49:24 etc.), to be set beside the later smashing of the golden calf. There are relics of a time when God commanded and accepted human sacrifice, including child sacrifice, together with God's later attempts to distance himself from this very unfortunate fact about his past history. Finally, there are many occasions when God appears amongst humans in human form, or sits enthroned in Heaven just like a human king surrounded by his courtiers, to be set beside the later general prohibition of imagery, and the exalted, purely transcendent God-beyond-images of the Second Isaiah. Even that high theology is not the end of the story, for in Genesis itself there is secular-humanist prose fiction to anticipate what we will later meet in the Court History of David. Also in Genesis, we find a man like Abraham, who can be sufficiently advanced to challenge God to his face with a boldness that impressed even Nietzsche, and looks forward to the scepticism of Ecclesiastes and others of the biblical Writings.

The Hebrew Bible, incidentally, is very varied. It contains four groups of books: the Law, the Former Prophets, the Latter Prophets, and the Writings—the Psalms and the books of wisdom. The old Augustine-to-Calvin Grand Narrative tried to squeeze all this variety into a single orthodox systematic theology, which was completely mistaken. Instead, we'll take advantage of all that biblical diversity in telling our new Grand Narrative of the birth, the life, the death and the afterlife of God, and of how, through this great story of his own progressive development and his own self-emptying, God gave us all our basic ideas about ourselves and the world, and in the end died to complete his work of creating us.

In short, the God of the Hebrew Bible is in almost continuous self-transformation, and recapitulates in himself the entire history of religions—a history in which every one of us is still caught up, a history which we still somehow communicate to our children in their bedtime stories, and the history of how we came to be ourselves.

A turning-point in the whole story is the moment—already mentioned, above—when a people who have always been nomadic hunter-gatherers and pastoralists decide to settle down and become farmers.[7]

The change is enormous, eventually transforming almost every aspect of culture. For example, the pastoralist in very hot countries often prefers to move his flocks by night, or at least when the sun is not at its hottest. He will tend to measure time in terms of moons, the moons or months of animal and human "menses" and pregnancies. Eastern shepherds like moons. But the settled farmer lives by the sun and by the annual agricultural cycle of tasks, which are marked out and drilled into him by a Calendar and a round of festivals laid down by the priests in the Temple in the City. Settling down, or "civilization," marks the beginning of the timetabling of life from the Centre. Farmers need markets, and farming life tends to become highly routinized. The farm does not exist *alone*: it exists in relation to a great Centre—nowadays a "CBD"—where the god sits in his Temple on one side of the market place, and the King anointed by him sits in his palace on another side. To the Temple the farmer takes his produce, and in the Temple it is received in exchange for money—the words "money" and "mint" deriving from the Temple of Juno Moneta in Rome, because it was the god who originally invented the cash economy, minting the coins with her own image stamped upon them to guarantee them, and putting a raised rim— and maybe also, milling—around their edges in order to stop people from clipping them. Yes, the gods invented *everything*, and especially they were concerned about commutative justice, nowadays called business ethics. The entire system of settled life in the emergent city-state is theological, having been designed by priests who speak for gods. By the priests, agri*cult*ure, religious *cult*, and *cult*ure were all woven together. And in particular, God invented markets, money and fair trade. God invented "centred" life, and the city-state: politics, routine, law, and taxation. The first taxes, tithes, were paid to God the first Landlord.

It had to be this way. In the past God had lived in a portable tent, and during their long march through the wilderness he had marched daily at the head of his people in a pillar of cloud by day and a pillar of fire by night. But now God was minded to settle down. He didn't *have* to be a homeless wanderer: he owned all lands and all livestock, and his ownership was more than just a matter of traditional seasonal grazing-rights. It was absolute ownership. So God had chosen a territory, and had chosen a city to settle in. He would give his people the power to conquer and settle the land. He was already dictating to Moses the code of sacred Law by which the people would live when they got there.

In the new Holy Land, questions of land tenure would be very important. God would be the sovereign lawgiver and proprietor, and the Temple would be the seat of his power, its college of priests administering his property on his behalf. Eventually, a king would take over from them.

The system I am describing has been amazingly influential and durable. Though most of us know it best from the Bible, it was already taking shape in Mesopotamia in the fourth millennium BCE, and eloquent relics of it are still to be seen in the parish church at Brookland, West Kent— perhaps the last place of worship still in use anywhere in the world that is fully equipped to function as a storehouse for agricultural produce. (In Britain, the final abolition of tithes has only just been completed!)

Under the old system the tenure of land comes down from God, through the monarch, to various sorts of freeholders and tenants. Farm workers might be in various ways "bound" to the land, or might be day-labourers or slaves.

As for the land and the two sexes, one need only consider the interestingly-profound differences between *patrimony* and *matrimony*. The transition from nomadism to farming and taking your produce to the City which centred and regulated your life and protected you was a transition to a new social order in which the ordinary peasant-farmer's chief ambition in life was to hand over intact to his son the property that he had inherited from his father. Woman was bound in matrimony to man in order to help man to maintain and hand over his patrimony. That's how it was. Don't blame me, dear.

Without going into any more detail, the settled farmer's new way of life involved a vast and complex transformation of the whole of culture. It made everything different, to such an extent that the mutual antagonism and incomprehension between travellers and settled people persists to this day—for example in Eastern European attitudes to Roma, or "gypsies." One simply cannot imagine ancient wanderers considering all the pros and cons, and deciding by themselves to embark upon such a momentous transition. They didn't have and could not invent the settled man's notion of land ownership. They would only become capable of that kind of thinking *after* they had gone through the change. They needed slowly to be taught all the new concepts. So, as it had been since the very beginning of the human story, God had to lead the way, taking the decision, telling them what it would involve, and dragging them reluctantly into the new epoch. Even then, according to the Hebrew Bible, there remained an obstinate group of conservatives, the Rechabites, who insisted upon continuing to live in tents and refused to eat cereals or to drink wine (vineyards and viticulture being to nomads a great symbol of the moral dangers of civilization). Even though he himself has taken the opposite point of view, God finds himself compelled to admire them (Jeremiah 35; see vv. 18f.)! In retrospect, the Israelites themselves freely acknowledged that they had not by themselves opted for civilization: "A wandering Aramaean [scil., "a mere nobody"] was my father, and he went down into Egypt . . . the Lord brought us out of Egypt . . . he brought us into this place and gave us this land" (Deuteronomy 26:5ff.).

The general point being made at this stage of the whole argument is that before the rise of philosophy and, still more, before the rise of a settled city life and a literate culture, human existence was not yet sufficiently *centred*, settled, stabilized and regulated for there to be any developed conception either of an autonomous human self or of a relatively autonomous natural order. Only when life has become settled around a fixed centre can one begin to think of God as one, and as a lawgiver. *Then* one can develop more unified, regularized conceptions of the cosmic and social orders and, in time, of the self.

Everything had to be thought *via* the supernatural order, or *via* God. God had at every point to take the lead and show the way. I couldn't *think out* anything for myself: I had to call upon God's spirit or God's wisdom to illuminate my mind. I couldn't *innovate*: God alone innovated. I couldn't work out my own *values*: I needed to be taught God's revealed will and to obey it. And the world?—it was not yet the relatively-independent, law-governed and predictable natural order that Aristotle was to declare it to be: it was "the garment of God," and its only ordering principle was God's word, and his faithfulness to his own promises.

So in everything God had to lead the way—and did so, but with an extraordinary corollary in that as "culture" develops the God of the Bible progressively transfers his powers to us, building us up and fading out himself. By his own slow self-emptying even unto death, God progressively creates us human beings. At first, theology was the Queen of the sciences, in the sense that almost the *whole* of our ideal culture was religious; but then God very gradually conceals his own person and withdraws. He makes an early start by handing power over animals even to Adam, and the power of procreation, with all that comes with it, to the pair, Adam-and-Eve. He knows that eventually he's going to have to hand over *knowledge,* and in particular the power to create even morality itself; but he doesn't want to hurry. He needs to hang on for a while to his power to rule our behaviour. In the meanwhile, he begins to organize his own gradual disappearance.

First, he stops appearing in person, in human form, as a man who walks among men. His last appearances in this mode, to Abraham and to Jacob, are already somewhat veiled. Thereafter, he continues to be seen, but only in very formalized contexts, and with due regard for precedence. Only Moses can see God frequently: the remainder—

Aaron, his sons Nadab and Abihu, and the seventy elders—have to remain at a distance, apart from the one memorable occasion when the entire delegation call formally upon God in heaven, walking out over the blue glass of the sky, and being entertained with food and drink (Exodus 24:1f., 9ff.). Thereafter God is seen directly only in call-visions, often associated with his official earthly residence, the Temple. He is surrounded by blinding light.

Later still, as social life becomes gradually more routinized and regularized, God as an individual person tends to become veiled behind the working of his own revealed Law—just as in our own society people speak of *faceless* bureaucrats. If the Law is working well, no personal interventions by the Lawgiver himself should be necessary. It is sufficient to have a body of professional scribes, interpreters of the Law, and judges who between them maintain the rule of Law. God seems already to be fading away. So long as the religious system continues to work satisfactorily, he can disappear behind it. It can work by itself, and God is not needed.

However, Israel became slack, negligent, and fell into sin. As always, older people felt that the young were becoming undisciplined, and harked back to the good old days when authority was respected, and those who broke the rules received swift and summary punishment. Disasters and national defeat prompted talk of a broken covenant. How was religion to be renewed? Just law, by itself, was apparently not sufficient to change obdurate, wilful human nature. A return to something like the old immediacy was required, but how?

Once again, the initiative had to come from God himself. Israel was a naughty schoolboy who had been in a disciplinary relationship to God, *via* a Law imposed upon him from above; and like any other schoolboy he had broken the Law "because it was there." It was time to move on to a more adult relationship to God—which meant restoring immediacy, which meant closing the gap between the springs of action in the human heart and its Other, the Good, the divine will. In effect, God must be internalized within "man," to make us fully autonomous.

The Israelite prophets used various metaphors at this point. God would pour out his Spirit upon all flesh, God would take away our hearts of stone and give us hearts of flesh, God would write his law directly upon our hearts, God would relocate from the Temple to the individual human heart, and God would become entirely immanent within us, indwelling us.

In short, the prophets looked for a radical *democratization* of God, of the sort that after the protestant Reformation was achieved partly in Congregationalism, and most fully in the Society of Friends (Quakers). God would no longer be an objective being, an absolute monarch over against us. Instead, God would be scattered into individual human hearts, just as in liberal democracy sovereignty is not external, but is distributed amongst all the people. The resulting society would be egalitarian: neither hierarchy—that is, the government of society by a college of priests—nor a caste or class system would any longer be necessary. Everybody would be as close to God as it is possible to be, God and the individual human self having become fully concentric. There would be no religion anymore, because religion is an apparatus of mediation between the individual human being and a god who is perceived as being exalted and distant. When God and the self coincide, the Law ends, religion ends, and in effect *God* ends too.

All this implies that already in the greatest Israelite prophets, the final revelation of God will be also the death of God, the final disappearance of God as a distinct being. Not quite "atheism" in our modern sense, but something more like "anthropomonism" or "hominism."

5

GOD, A TRANSITIONAL
OBJECT?

We need to recapitulate the argument, so that as we run up to the crux or climax of the new Grand Narrative we are clear about where we are and what is at stake.

We began by recognizing that in a post-Darwinian, secular and pragmatic age, our own world, the human life-world, the world that exists in our speech about it and consciousness of it, is the only "real" world we know of or have any evidence for. We don't know for sure of anyone else who has a world at all, and as for ourselves, we are always inside our own human angle on our own world. Many animals clearly have some ability to project out little worlds around themselves. They may be territorial, social and communicative; but animals do not alter their environment to anything like the extent that we do, and their worlds seem to be no more than reduced versions of our world. We look at them retrospectively, even *nostalgically*, because they give us a glimpse of where we came from; but their little worlds do not seriously challenge or rival our own. As for the very large-scale physical cosmology that has been developed by modern physics, it is a theoretical construct, a *supplement*, projected out from within our own human life-world, and checked back against it. Much of the great thirteen-billion-year history it recounts is in principle unobserved and unobservable by anyone: there never was and there isn't now a standpoint from anybody could ever observe "Big Bangs" and "black holes." They may be, and no doubt they *are*, very useful theoretical entities, but they are not "real" for us in the way that *our* world, the human life world, that is, the world of our language is. The world is our setting-in-life, our own *milieu*. It is only transient, it is our own accumulated construct, but it's what there is. It's primary. Scientists do not escape it: on the contrary, they live inside it, just as the rest of us do.

A consequence of this is that a new Grand Narrative religious story about how we began, how we have become what we are, what there is for us, and how we should live—any such Great Story today must take the form of a history of our human ideal culture—a history of mind, of consciousness, of language, of our own evolving under-standing of ourselves and our world. The first great phi-losopher to grasp this was Hegel, and I am here attempting in a very sober, low-key, and mediocre English way to go over at least some of the ground he first covered in *The Phenomenology of Spirit*, 1805. Hegel was the first to see that if the world is our world, and if the human mind is the only site from which there has ever been any attempt to build a complete world and understand it, then the history of hu-man thought coincides with and is the history of "reality" as a whole, the history of Everything. We are the world-builders. Only *we* have built a really big world-picture and as I am saying, our world-picture is, in effect, just the world. We cannot distinguish clearly between the world as it is in our current conversation and the world as it is absolutely. There's only our world, namely our own current world-view. There is only our "angle."

It follows that anyone like me who is so unwise as to wish to get Christianity up-to-date needs to replace the old Western-Christian Grand Narrative theology with a new story, a history of human thought that will show how we managed to evolve out of our animal background, and why our ideal culture, the programming in our heads, was and *had* to be religious for so long. As I am telling it, the whole human story is turning out to be the story of the birth, the life, the death and the afterlife of the gods and God. Through telling the story, we may get a little clearer about ourselves and our situation, and we may also become a little clearer about the sort of "reality" God used to have—and also his status now, in his afterlife period.

The earliest humans then began as animals, with the animal's very low level of consciousness, and in a darkness illuminated only by sharp, stabbing flashes of alarm or excitement when something biologically-significant loomed up. The animal has a biologically built-in ability to identify the stimulus—it's one of our chief predators, it's a potential rival of the same sex, it's a potential mate, of the opposite sex and in season, it is something that threatens my young, and so on—and the stimulus triggers off the appropriate behavioural response. The animal is completely immersed in its own life, always alert and always engagé. It has no problem about doing its own thing.

The early human is not quite the same, because humans early in their development took the unusual path of rather extreme neoteny (Greek, meaning roughly "extended immaturity"). The human body remains relatively hairless, unspecialized, and immature-looking, for a human at birth resembles other mammals in embryo. Its chief distinguishing feature is a relatively oversized, but still rather undeveloped, brain. Thus, whereas many animals have to be able to get up and run with the herd an hour or two after birth, a human is quite helpless and requires many years of nursing, training and education before it can fend for itself. When we recall that the average human expectation of life at birth, during nearly all of human history before 1800 CE or so, was below 30 years, we realize with a shock that being young yourself and then raising *your own* young used to take up virtually the whole of your life. You were immature until about fourteen, then married and raised your own young, and then counted yourself fortunate if you had lived long enough to see "your children's children and peace upon Israel" (as the Bible puts it) before you died. Most of life was *tradition*: you were taught, and then you handed on what you had been taught. You lived in order to pass on life itself, and your people's cultural tradition.

In human beings, culture, tradition, language, and consciousness itself are all one streaming communal process, Hegel's "Geist," in a way that makes our relation to our own experience different from the animal's. Domesticated and captive animals are dull, sad things, but the true "wild" animal, seen in the wild, is prodigiously keyed-up, vital, alert, and quick to respond. I look at it admiringly, because as a human I am distanced a little from my own experience by my own possession of language and consciousness. That little distancing or standing-back from immediacy I call *"minding."* It is the space of hesitation, anxiety, reflection. In that space we remember similar previous occasions, review many different possible hypotheses, and have our doubts. We take our time; but we may take too much time, suffer from paralyzing anxiety, and find it impossible to commit ourselves wholeheartedly to one course of action. As the idiom has it, we "mind" too much. "**I am at my wits' end**," we say, "What am I to do?"—two amongst a wide range of idioms that indicate how important it is, in a demanding situation, to **gather your wits**, to **keep your wits about you**, and not to become **scared out of your wits**.

How was the early human being to cope with this? His high level of consciousness ought to be biologically advantageous, but it threatens to be disabling.

The life-world presented itself to him as a theatre in which mysterious violent forces contested against each other, and sometimes turned against him abruptly. How was he, or she, ever to achieve any kind of mastery of his own life and of his world? He knew and understood almost nothing. In particular, he needed to cope with sudden biologically-significant presentations, as I have called them. He needed instantly to classify them correctly and to respond appropriately.

The most vivid and obviously-important example of this is the appearance of a fellow animal who must be recognized very promptly as the prey-animal that we are hunting for, or as one of the predators that we have most reason to fear, or whatever. In each case, I need to have firmly lodged in my mind a guiding, standard image of the kind, the type, the species, the Universal, so that I can hold it up before me and recognize at once when something that falls into this class presents itself.

This standard universal is what students of religion call the Totem, philosophers call the Universal or the (platonic) Form, and a modern biologist may call simply the species. I suggested earlier that surviving cave-paintings and other very early art-works show that among hunter-gatherers a typical religious ritual was one that had the function of preparing men for the hunt. It impressed upon all their minds a standard guiding image of the particular species of animal that they were to look out for, and it did this with great force, so that during the hunt as soon as one of the hunters spotted the prey the whole group were very quickly galvanized into effective collective action.

This I take to be a very simple model of the earliest form of religion. It is already communal, it involves ritual, and it employs various means such as music, dance, special dress, and mild intoxicants of plant origin, which combine to make the participants suggestible. The proceedings may be led by a religious professional, the shaman, and his function is to bind the participants together. Their attention becomes intensely focussed upon the religious object in a way that equips them to set forth upon a very-important collective enterprise, and *stay* focussed.

The religious object upon which people learn to focus is a universal guiding image which helps us to interpret experience and to succeed in life. It shows us how to live. It is culture's replacement for the animal's quick built-in reflex response to a sudden stimulus or an urgent need. It is the *sign*, or in modern jargon the iconic example.

Is it not rather cumbrous? you may ask. An animal has no problem in doing straight off what an animal of its species has got to do, but we humans, we make heavy weather of life, we are anxiety-ridden and we have only a very short attention span. We need ritual, dressing up, communal training, and religious imagery to help us to focus and to stay focussed upon the major communal enterprises that our life requires of us. I gave the hunt as an example, but I might perhaps have cited an initiation-ceremony, or a wedding, or rituals to do with war or rain.

At any rate, I suggest that the totem may be taken as the forerunner of what will in due course become the "spirit" and then the god. The whole system of totems recognized by a particular tribe is an early classification of the environment, highlighting especially items that you need to look out for. Combined with ritual and the special mental states associated with it, the system of totems soon evolves into the spirit-world. How? Because the Universal, the general word, is ideal, and not empirical. It is authoritative and powerful, it is not part of the world of mortal things, and it gets into your head. During the earliest stages of settled life the spirits become gods, but as tribes confederate to form the first state societies the gods do not entirely forget their animal origins. In ancient Egypt they retained their animal heads, and in every religion (except perhaps Islam) animal symbolism remains surprisingly prominent even to this day. For Christians, Christ is still a Lamb, or a Lion, and the Spirit a Dove.

Why—for example, during the formation of the ancient Egyptian state—do the totem-animals become spirits and then gods, cosmic giants, beings far exalted above us in their greatness and power? Presumably they are teaching us to think on a larger and larger scale. We die, our kings die; but the Universal Kind, the totem, the Spirit, the God, and the State—they live on forever. We are developing an ordered cosmology, and a large-scale state society which claims cosmic validation for its permanent authority over us. Thought is becoming more unified. The old World Tree is becoming the new *axis mundi*, around which the world turns. The cosmos and the state are becoming ordered, rational, unified. God is gradually becoming One, a cosmic lawgiver, an all-round regulator of the world and of our lives. Scholars systematize the body of religious Law, expecting it to be one as the God is one. So now, as God, the world, the monarch, the state and religious Law are all becoming one, the human self at last and belatedly becomes more unified.

In traditional marxizing theories the material basis of life comes first, and then practices, movements and conflicts at the material level come to be reflected in society's ideal culture. All our religious and related beliefs are epiphenomena, mere froth. My story reverses the order, suggesting instead that religious objects and ideas are always *leading* ideas. They are ideal, normative, standard-setting ideas, picking out important features of our environment and showing us how to cope with them, guiding us through life towards an ideal order that always remains somewhat ahead of us.

In our religious thought, therefore, God leads the way in showing us what to become and how to live. Thus in Israel, as in the Mesopotamian city-states, kingship and lawgiving *started* with the gods, and only gradually was the god persuaded to delegate these functions to a human king who would act for him and in his name. Religion was long a socially-progressive force: God was an indirect, heterological way of thinking about, and of seeing yourself as commanded to march forward into, a future that you could scarcely yet imagine. And by being constantly on the move, and growing ever-bigger himself, God continually raised the bar, inducing us to aim higher. I am therefore suggesting that we should drop the popular idea of God as an infinite, perfect and unchanging Being, and instead see God as evolving somewhat ahead of us, as a carrot, a dream, a guiding star. God *leads* human development. He is in perpetual metamorphosis, and in his self-transformations keeps a step or two ahead of us.

This way of thinking about God was introduced by Hegel, and of course it has not yet caught on with the general public. But it gives us a way of continuing to see religion as important, and as having been necessary to our development until quite recently, in a culture that is now secular, humanistic, and historicist in its world-view. We should be grateful to God: he created us.

The question now arises of what status we should ascribe to these "necessary myths." In a book called *Playing and Reality*, the British psychologist D. W. Winnicott long ago introduced the idea of a "transitional object."[8] It is an object of uncertain status, real to the infant who is fiercely attached to it, but perhaps fictional in the eyes of an observer. It helps the child to get through a difficult period. It is an imaginary friend and companion, a comfort blanket, a favourite doll, even perhaps a guardian angel, a tutelary spirit. Other words used are fetish, talisman, mascot and charm.

The ambiguous status of the transitional object may remind us that Plato's Forms were to him real beings, subsisting in a higher, intelligible world; whereas for Aristotle the

Forms are just useful ideas in our heads, or even—in later thought—just general *words*, universal terms that we use to classify items in our environment.

Is God, or was God, some such transitional object, that was at first necessary to life, and then later, as human cultural life developed, became steadily more exalted, and finally disappeared into redundant obscurity? Might we be ready now to replace the word "God" with a more modern word such as "language" or "culture"? In which case we may look back on religion as an institution that was necessary, progressive, and very valuable to us in its day, but nowadays is simply not needed any more.

Hum. We do not need to do more at this stage of the argument than simply to bear that suggestion in mind.

6

OTHER PEOPLE'S BELIEFS

Energetic and omnivorously interested in everything, the Victorian British collected and sent back home large quantities of reports about the customs and beliefs of the many peoples who had recently had the good fortune to become subjects of the Great White Queen over the Seas. The beliefs seemed very exotic, and so were the corresponding items of material culture that were also arriving. But few doubted that the beliefs, at least, could be clearly understood and evaluated. The religious beliefs of savages were judged to be simply false hypotheses about the world, and with the spread of European Enlightenment they would naturally wither away. Meanwhile, the chief task of academic anthropology was to explain how such odd beliefs had come to be held, and why they had been clung to so tenaciously for so long in the absence of any solid evidence for their truth. The best book along these lines was probably Sir Edward Tylor's *Primitive Culture*, 1871.

The figures most important in pointing out the weakness of the Victorian approach and showing a better way were Emile Durkheim and Bronislaw Malinowski. They insisted that a people's religious beliefs are intimately bound up with their whole culture, and need to be understood as if from within. The new anthropologists' method of "participant observation" involved what the Victorians would have called "going native," and indeed doing so in a very big way—learning the language, living amongst the people for at least one whole year, becoming totally immersed in their life, and recording everything. The more fully the student described the way the beliefs functioned in their own setting-in-social-life, the easier it would be to understand them correctly.

In good hands, such as those of the British anthropologist E. E. Evans-Pritchard, the method produced some excellent studies.[9] But by the 1960s problems were beginning to pile up. Decolonization was making it harder to place young research students safely, especially after some of them had become militant advocates who were battling to defend the people they studied against encroaching loggers, and even against their own governments. Others said that the method of study involved a colonialism of the mind, which swallowed an ancient culture whole and laid it out cold in a display case in Western academia's imaginary museum. Durkheim's famous statement that "all religions are true" came to be seen as resembling Wittgenstein's dictum that "this language-game is played": any religious system that is practised is true—but only in a very reduced, positivistic sense. It's just *there*: it is done. That's all that can be said.

More serious still, Victorian agnostics and unbelievers might hold that tribal beliefs were obviously false; but they had no trouble with their *meaningfulness*, because they were familiar with religious belief in their own society. Even as late as Evans-Pritchard, you could still see that the reason why he was so successful in making East African religious beliefs seem intelligible was that he had become a Roman Catholic convert himself. But to anthropologists more consistently secular, critical and modern than Evans-Pritchard, traditional African (and still more, Australian and Papuan) world-views were becoming quite unintelligible. By about 1970, anthropologists such as Rodney Needham were beginning to feel that we can never fully make our own the minds of people so utterly different from ourselves. The huge surge of higher education, and of science and technology, in the modern West has greatly accelerated the long-term decline of religion, making it harder and harder for us to empathize with archaic and fully mythico-religious ways of thinking that have now slipped further and further away from us, into our past. It has happened to *me*, even though I am technically still a priest. Back in the nineteen-fifties I still felt pretty sure that I understood clearly what God is supposed to be, what a spirit is supposed to be, and what the supernatural world, the abode of the dead, is supposed to be. I might already have doubts, but at least I didn't doubt that I understood what it was that I doubted. Whereas today . . .

Many of the humanities are currently very painfully aware of the difficulty I am describing, but in one subject there has been an interesting fightback. Archaeology may be a small subject, but it has a large lay public who are keen to hear all about human origins, and about human development during the prehistoric period. How did consciousness begin, and how did language begin? "Cognitive archaeology" has argued persuasively that one can draw inferences about world-view and about beliefs from *non-literary*, prehistoric evidence, and writers such as Colin Renfrew, Steven Mithen and David West-Williams have been able to find large readerships for their books.

I greatly admire their work, but I cannot quite write as they do because of my philosophical reservations. It seems to me beyond doubt that traditional religious belief and ways of thinking are fast disappearing entirely. If religion can survive at all, it can survive today only in very reduced and corrupt form, as something like militant, puritanical, and anti-liberal ethnonationalism. Nobody can say clearly any longer what they suppose God to be, what they suppose a spirit to be, what they suppose the abode of the dead to be (or where it is), what they suppose divine action to be, or what they suppose the religious life to be and how they might pursue it today. For this reason, I find it hard simply to accept accounts of shamans transformed into birds or canoeing around remote cosmic regions. A family member catching me "lost in thought" may laugh at me for being "miles away"—but I really cannot credit the shaman with anything more than that. What *is* he saying?

In short, we have to reckon with a much more complete secularization of culture than has so far been envisaged. The main reason for it is that the culture is now completely dominated by science and technology, which ever since the 1660s have been committed to very strict rules for the meaningful and truth-telling use of language. As a result, all the old high and grand rhetorical styles have been lost: think of what has happened to epic poetry and to tragedy. The cosmology of modern natural science, remarkable though it is, can tell us nothing about ourselves, nothing about religion or ethics or politics or art, nor even about "life"—and yet it does not know and cannot tell what a desert it has created, and is still creating. With the death of epic and tragedy whole dimensions of life have been lost, and I don't see how we are going to get them back.

Mention of the strict rules for the use of language when writing a scientific report for publication reminds me of the way my own proposed fightback differs from that of the cognitive archaeologists. My thesis is that the only possible location today for the unseen supernatural world of religion, together with all its denizens and forces, is within the neglected and little-understood world of linguistic meaning. When I am "lost in thought," I am listening to language idling, moving spontaneously in my own head.

This idea has a long history and I have myself been playing with it for many years. Plato's Intelligible World of the Forms looks very like a philosophical rationalization of the spirit-world of popular religious belief. The Forms are timeless, potent, archetypal, and they shape our thinking.

For Plato himself, the Forms seem to be objectively-existing beings. For Aristotle, they are concepts in our minds, and for the mediaeval nominalists they are just *nomina* (= words). But in Christian Platonism the whole world of Forms tends to become enclosed within the Divine Mind, and the Forms are redescribed as the Divine Ideas, the archetypes of all created things. Alternatively, the Forms—especially the most powerful ones—may be seen as angels, or as the divine energies.

To take Christian Platonism further: when monotheism is firmly held and God is strong, he unifies and keeps firm control over the whole world of Ideas/Angels. The word "God" becomes a master-word that keeps the whole of language "centred" and in place. There is often a line between "clean" and "dirty" or "bad" language, and, again, under normal conditions when God is strong and language is under firm disciplinary control all the bad/rebellious words or angels are firmly excluded from linguistic heaven. They are confined to an underworld that no decent person visits or even mentions. No "foul language" is allowed to erupt. But in the time of the death of God linguistic discipline breaks down, and all the most powerful angels/words break loose and rampage wildly through the world—as, of course, happens in Iris Murdoch's novel *The Time of the Angels*, which is about the religious crisis of the 1960s. Everything becomes "disinhibited."

These ideas have swirled around the edges of philosophical Platonism for two millennia. Here I point only to the rough correspondence between Plato's Forms, Aristotle's Concepts, the Angelic Hierarchies, the Divine Ideas and general words/abstract nouns as the ideal archetypes or exemplars of particular actual things in the world. These ideas are all interrelated and they show us how we might possibly recover some lost dimensions of life if we were to pay more attention to the mysterious, magical and little-understood world of linguistic meaning.

What guides have we? The best single intellectual tradition available to us for opening up the area is that of Freud, Lacan and Derrida, and associated writers. Lacan set aside Freud's own claim to be a scientist, and instead treated Freud as a brilliant interpreter of our symbolic behaviour, and of language. Derrida is sometimes outstandingly original and illuminating. In addition, now that the guardians of his legacy are allowing the publication of more of his remains, it is possible that the work of Carl Jung—and of some of his followers, such as Joseph Campbell and Mircea Eliade—may have a contribution to make. But the only general thesis I offer at this stage in the argument is that a richer philosophy of language/writing/symbolism may help us to understand better and in more detail the long history of religious thought out of which we have come to be what we now are.

7

MEDIATED RELIGION

Our new Grand Narrative theology is a drama in four acts or dispensations.

Act One of the drama, in chapter 3 above, described how it all began. At first, before they developed language, our remote ancestors lived in a foaming darkness lit by occasional sharp flashes and stabs of pleasure or pain, but as yet unilluminated by language. They had no conscious, organized, centred selfhood, and no centred, organized world. Their foaming darkness was temporal, but their time was not yet linear, for you need sentences to give you the idea of one-way linear time. In fact, they needed common nouns and verbs—that is, some beginnings of substance and causality—before they could even begin to have a world. All that they had in their favour was their own urgent need to survive and their relative immaturity, which gave them the need and the ability to learn a lot, fast.

They learned to make two distinctions. First, they learnt to classify the particulars in their environment of most importance to them into kinds. They did this by fixing before their eyes a picture of the kind, a standard example of the kind of creature that they must hunt, or flee from, or do business with. This object, in their minds, might be called a concept. On their lips, it was a common noun, like "gazelle," or "lion." In their religion, it might be called a totem.

A philosopher might call it a universal, meaning a general word, with an unrestricted range of possible applications.

The ability accurately to identify in the environment an individual thing as belonging to some important class was so vital that your whole society might be divided up into totem groups, each having as its mascot one totem in the tribe's whole system of totems. Individual persons might carry a wooden or stone symbol of their own totem. In this way society as a whole was a kind of living library, reflecting in its structure the structure of its environment.

So much for the origin of knowledge and of nouns (= *nomina*, = general "names"). The second primitive distinction was that between a thing's motion and the cause of its motion (maybe wind, maybe breath, maybe a hidden predator stalking me). Here perhaps is the location of our very first enquiries about causality, and our first use of verbs.

I have also suggested that even before anybody has a self or is self-aware, it may be possible to recognize in chaotic experience the existence of the standpoint of the subject to whom this chaos is present.

Now let us consider the status of the universal term, the Totem, the exemplar. It is not itself part of the world of mortal creatures. Each and every actual gazelle will die, but gazellehood, the standard universal Gazelle, does not die. It is not in time at all. It is before our eyes, between us and our world, so that we use it as a template to help us to identify a particular creature as a gazelle. So it is *leading*, it is *powerful*, it is sort-of in our heads, we need to keep our attention fixed on it . . . in short, the totem is on the way to being a spirit. People may in their religion sacrifice it in order to share its life and to "commune" with it.[10] A very late illustration of the principle is the use of "Lamb of God" as a title of Jesus in the Eucharistic liturgy: he is "Agnus Dei."

Enough: now for Act Two, in chapter 4 above. We sketched the enormous cultural changes that took place as, after the last Ice Age, our ancestors gradually settled down to become farmers and citizens in a state society. Farmers have needs: they needed military protection against marauding bands, they needed law and order to settle disputes about tenure, boundaries, and inheritance, they needed markets where they could be sure of a fair price for their produce, and they even needed a Calendar timetabling the annual round of agricultural tasks. Better still, they would like to have specialist craftsmen to supply them with tools, pottery, textiles and the like. In fact they needed to have a city to look to, a king to fight their wars for them, and a god enthroned in the city to sustain and regulate their whole lives. Like any other businessmen with goods to trade, the farmers wanted peace, but peace in a land of perpetually warring city-states comes at a heavy price. The Israelites in the Bible couldn't say they were not warned: "A king? He'll tax you heavily to pay for his building projects. He'll conscript your sons for forced labour and for his army, and he'll have your daughters to be his perfumers and his cooks. You'll be his slaves. You want a *king*?" On the whole, yes, they did. Well, most of them did (see 1 Samuel 8).

The grandiose ideology that eventually developed in the Bronze and early-Iron Age civilizations is familiar around the world as well as in the Bible. Versions of it survived until very recently in Moscow and Beijing, in Tokyo and Addis Ababa, in Lhasa and in Istanbul—religiously-validated absolute monarchy was not at all fussy about which religion it used, just so long as it got itself duly validated. But we should note that the more the supernatural world is centred in One God, and the more the cosmos is seen on the analogy of the state, with a long long chain of command rising vertically above the ordinary person's head, the more strictly disciplined everyone is. In a fully-developed state society, with divine or at least "anointed" sacred kingship, religion comes to be seen as above all a matter of *law*.

Nobody has the sort of freedom a rich nomad like Abraham had once enjoyed. Everyone in state society is more-or-less locked into his place in the system, and everyone is the prisoner of his own rank—even if he is the King or the Pope. You may admire the religious and artistic splendour of the system, and the magnificent works of art that celebrated it, but who really wants to live a life as highly-regulated as that? Even if you personally passionately believe in the system as divinely instituted, it remains liable to sudden falsification by military defeat or by political breakdown, and the literatures of ancient Egypt and Mesopotamia testify to how traumatic such a collapse of his world could be for the ordinary person—a scribe perhaps, literate, but now forever hopelessly redundant.[11]

In the developed system of mediated religion a new type of religious professional becomes prominent. He is a learned, literate man, a *clerus*, clerk or cleric, who is sometimes but not always a priest. Every member of his order or rank can be relied upon to wear black, and to be equipped with a standard body of religious knowledge and ritual skills. He has an interest in cosmology, because he helps to determine and publish the religious and civic Calendar. (The Pope and the Queen still have their own astronomers and observatories.) In addition, the religious professionals have a strong interest in the interpretation of the sacred scriptures, and in the publication and administration of religious law.

Religion of the kind I am describing tends with the passage of time to become ever more codified (i.e., made bookish), elaborated, and routinized. The body of sacred writings gets bigger and bigger—not least, in Hinduism and Buddhism. The number of religious professionals and the splendour of religious architecture grow exponentially. Eventually, the system of mediated religion becomes an end in itself, and forgets what it was originally *for*. In fact, its chief interest comes to be in its own survival. In the beginning it had been profitable to the self, because it gave us a more stable, regularized, settled life in a more orderly world. But in the end life comes to be dominated by religious Law. Ethics for most is just obedience, service, and admiration for the great ones above you.

Meanwhile, the older type of religious professional—the charismatic, imaginative individual shaman or prophet—is not quite extinct. He—or she, it may be—still crops up occasionally as a lay mystic, visionary or poet. The best-loved modern English example of the type is the eccentric artist-poet William Blake (1757–1827). In religion, as elsewhere, standardization is usually equated with sanity, and individuality with madness. Blake is no exception: we see the uniformed orthodox cleric as sane, and Blake as crazy, but we are also fascinated by his flashes of top-level poetic genius. He gives us a suggestion that religion might become less ready-made, might instead give us the imaginative power to transform, to transfigure reality and ourselves.

In antiquity, protest against the ultra-political, cosmology-based, overmanned, irrational and oppressive religions of early state societies becomes very important from about the seventh century BCE. Act Three of our new Grand Narrative theology begins therefore with the rise of *the individual*, who in different settings might appear as a sage, a prophet or a philosopher.

To take the *sages* first, evidences of high-quality individual speculative thought—often pessimistic and sceptical in tone—go back as far as early Middle-Kingdom Egypt, and are at first associated mainly with times of political—and therefore also religious—instability. Inevitably, texts that have reached us have come to us from intellectuals—literate people, scribes—who could leave us materials that we can read, in a form that has been able to survive. In late-Bronze and early Iron-Age times, the sage and his wisdom functioned chiefly to give counsel to kings. In a period of warring city-states and hot passions, kings needed cool and

rational disinterested advisors and administrators. Thus the
sage might be an advisor who also had the task of running
a school that trained younger men for public service. His
teachings would be conveyed in the form of proverbs, max-
ims and shrewd generalizations about human behaviour,
its motivation and its consequences. In particular, the sage
needed to inculcate enough self-knowledge and self-criti-
cism to protect his students against making potentially ru-
inous errors in politics (understood as *both* the management
of affairs within the state, *and* the management of relations
between states). In many ways, this kind of thinking is the
earliest critical thinking and the earliest secular thinking
that we know of: notice, in particular, that it probably *pre-
cedes* the rise of religious asceticism as a way to self-knowledge, self-mastery and self-improvement. This is a rare and
very important case in which religious history has been
profoundly influenced from "outside," and by a purely
secular style of thinking. By this I mean not only that the
cool, disciplined, impartial, self-critical and self-controlled
civil servant is the remote forerunner of the philosophers,
scientists, and other critical thinkers of later times, but also
that this particular mentality and style of thinking is of
very great value to religion itself. The historian of religions
Trevor Ling used to maintain that Buddhist spirituality had
first developed, and then in its early centuries functioned
principally, in just such a context. The Buddha reportedly
came from a princely family and taught the way to an ultra-
cool, unattached, and peaceable style of selfhood. The early
Buddhist monks sometimes functioned as counsellors, and
as tutors in princely houses. Hence Asoka, and Buddhism's
unexpectedly early "establishment."

Maybe Ling was right. The sages, culminating in the
Buddha, were mainly concerned to free men from the violent and self-destructive passions which raged in a world
of small and perpetually-warring city-states. The second
group of individual thinkers, namely the early *philosophers*,

directed their criticism mainly against the intellectually-absurd ideologies that the city-states had developed. Each regarded itself as being the centre of the world, each regarded its own gods as the true gods, its own layout and its own Sanctuary as being modelled upon a heavenly archetype, and its own religious law as the true cosmic law. The result was an extreme religious localism or "positivism" of a kind which is still familiar today, under the name of ethnonationalism. In an age of trade and travel, the observant thinker could not help but be struck by the remarkable variety of local beliefs and customs. Each independent city-state was a well with a few frogs at the bottom who all thought that their own well was the whole world. To escape from this kind of thinking the early philosophers sought to develop a secular and more rational philosophy of nature, a cosmic piety that venerated the cosmic order, and a moderate rational ethic that could claim to be in accord at least with *human* nature.

The third group of early intellectuals were the *prophets* of ethical monotheism, especially in early Israel. They looked back to the simplicity and freedom of the old nomadic way of life, and personally they somewhat resembled the charismatic shamans and oracles who had been its teachers. They were very critical of the corruption and general religious unsatisfactoriness of city-state life, and in particular of its Temple and its markets. They considered that the covenant was broken—interestingly, a vocabulary that our own modern politicians still use. But what did *they* mean by it, and what was the remedy?

The covenant was the bargain by which their ancestors had given up the old nomadic way of life in exchange for a more prosperous, rule-governed, and stable life under the protection of a God who would live permanently in a fixed sanctuary at the centre of the capital city. From this fixed sacred Centre the Calendar and the markets would be regulated, the currency would be issued and the law promulgated. The bargain was that the people would thus gain all the benefits of civilization, but in return they must be exclusively faithful to their god and obey his Law in full.

Now, the ideologies of the early civilizations were so constructed that if things went badly wrong it was never the god's fault, and it was always your fault. The god— or his priests, if you prefer—were very good at the blame game. If enemy forces raided and sacked your city, or if the harvest failed, the reason must be that you had been insufficiently observant. In response to each new crisis, the system must become ever more exacting and oppressive, until finally the prophets appear announcing that an entirely new covenant must be worked out, and God would announce its terms.

The main lines of the hoped-for reform are clear.[12] In developed society, as God had become more exalted and centred, he had become more remote. The ideology of the early state constructed reality as an enormous power-pyramid, with God at the very top, and Piers Plowman at the bottom, living the life of a serf. Indeed, the ancient state usually *was* a slave society, or at least a society that depended upon a variety of forms of serfdom and bonded labour. For the ordinary person God had disappeared behind a wall of impersonal and rigorously-enforced sacred Law. There needed to be a return of some form of religious immediacy. This in turn required *democratization*: God must decentre himself, coming down from heaven and distributing himself as spirit into human hearts. That, after all, was where religion had begun in hunter-gatherer times. The sacred world was before one's eyes all the time. One looked *through* it, so as by means of it to order and make sense of the life-world. Even the Arctic and the Australian desert could be seen as being, not barren, but full of stories and spirits *through* which people found their way around and made their lives liveable and rich. In religious ritual one slipped into a trance in order to give one's full attention to the supernatural order which was also one's own ideal culture, and which one was inside all the time.

So for the prophets God must come down from Heaven, decentring himself and distributing himself into every human heart as spirit. When God and the self have become concentric in this way, human beings will no longer be subject to an external code of law. They'll have "hearts of flesh," and will know how to live the good life expressively and spontaneously. They will have become religiously *non-dual*, and their life will be refreshed.

This longed-for future religious state eventually comes to be called "the Kingdom of God"; but note that it clearly implies the final disappearance of God from the external socially-constructed world. The old objective God of early state societies was a cosmic absolute Monarch. Politics loved him, but religion felt utterly alienated from him. Which is why the old mystical yearning for union with God was also a demand for the disappearance of God as objective being, as Other. Instead, God becomes at last fully and completely internalized.

8

THE END OF THE LAW

Jesus of Nazareth, in Galilee, was an itinerant Jewish teacher and reputed healer, who travelled around Palestine for a few years around the year 30 CE.[13]

That is about the end of what can be said about Jesus without significant disagreement, the sources for his life being numerous and of very uneven quality, and the religious interests at stake being very strong. Most—nearly all—scholars will agree however, that only *one* of the many witnesses, namely St John, supports the orthodox Christian view that in Jesus a pre-existent divine being became incarnate, and lived and died as a man. But by general consent St John's Jesus is so utterly different in his vocabulary and his message from the Jesus of Matthew, Mark and Luke that John has to be set aside. His Jesus is not the historical Jesus, and unless you hold the (strangely circular[14]) Catholic doctrine that God preserves the Church from doctrinal error, you must conclude that historic ecclesiastical faith is mistaken.

What then can be said about the message of the Jesus of Matthew, Mark, Luke, and (with some qualifications) Thomas? It seems to most scholars that Jesus himself did not claim to be the Messiah of the Jews. His core message was simply that "the Kingdom of God" was near, or had already arrived. The ancient prophetic hope was fulfilled. The divine world and the human life-world were at last coming together and becoming one. A new era had begun, and it was time to start living in a quite new way.

A consequence of the closing of the old gap between the two worlds, and of the old opposition between God and the individual human person, was that mediated religion, which hitherto had purported to bridge the gulf between God in Heaven and humans on earth, was now redundant. Indeed, Jesus was apparently very critical of most of it, and especially of the Temple, the various religious professionals, and the Law.

An even more momentous consequence of the new situation was that God had ceased to be an objective being. He had emptied himself out into human hearts. God and the human self were no longer two; they were now concentric. It followed that the difference between the pure and the impure, and between good and evil, was no longer imposed upon human beings "heteronomously"—that is, in the form of a code of divine laws revealed to Moses and received thenceforth from tradition—but depended solely upon the autonomous human heart. Living well was not a matter of keeping rules: on the contrary, rule-morality does not produce and never could produce the kind of person Jesus wanted to see. No: for Jesus—who in moral philosophy was a straight emotivist and expressivist—you live well if you live in a "solar" way, out from the heart, without any duplicity, so that your expressive life pours out upon a current of open, direct, generous and affirmative feeling. Jesus makes his point here by insisting that law-morality makes us mean-spirited. We are forever looking sideways at our neighbours, and feeling aggrieved if they are doing better than we think they deserve. He insists, paradoxically but brilliantly, that unless you are ready to go beyond mere justice and perform acts of ecstatic, excessive generosity, you are not a truly moral person *at all*.

A consequence of the new teaching was that Jesus was not in the popular sense a religious person. He does not have any teaching about sin and redemption, and he does not describe any itinerary or road map for the soul's long and arduous journey of self-purification into God. Unlike most Christians up to the time of Kierkegaard (and after), he is not an "amphibian"—a person who lives with one eye on this world and the other eye on the eternal world where God dwells. On the contrary, Jesus is purely secular and this-worldly in outlook. If he is religious at all, it is in the sense that he wants us to be wholly, selflessly and very directly given to the here and now.

In this, Jesus recalls various other teachers who have said something similar. In the Hellenistic culture of his day there was already an established notion of a divine man (*theios anēr*), a superior human being who is no longer under the yoke of religion but is free and fully adult, because he has wholly appropriated his own religion and now lives it out spontaneously, sinlessly, without effort, and purely affirmatively. The Bodhisattva in Buddhism is somewhat similar, and so are the New Man of Marxism and the Overman of Nietzsche.[15] The superior human being lives without *ressentiment* or reactive feeling: he is purely affirmative. He does not nurse any kind of grudge or ill-feeling.

How did Jesus' contemporaries receive his message? A few people must have liked it: otherwise his memory, and some of his words, would not have reached us at all. But the synoptic gospels do preserve a wide range of sharp criticism: he's mad, he's in league with the devil, he keeps bad company, he is lax about ritual purity and about the Sabbath, and he enjoys feasting. Some thought he had come to abolish the Law altogether, and regarded him as a "sorcerer" or as a false prophet who would lead Israel astray, a heretic, and even (eventually) an all-out blasphemer.

Since his followers are unlikely to have had any motive for inventing such an array of charges, they are quite probably historical, and from my point of view justified. Jesus was after all announcing the end of these people's world, and in many cases of their livelihoods. St. Matthew tries, rather absurdly, to claim that Jesus endorsed the Mosaic Law in full,[16] but the fact is that not long after Jesus' death the early Jewish Church did resolve *not* to impose the Law upon Gentile converts. The Church was thus in the position of claiming *both* to be the New Israel *and* to have moved into a new era after the end of the old system of religious mediation. The new, post-Torah religion continued to have a substantial Jewish membership and a broadly Jewish character in the East for two or three centuries, and to this day the Ethiopian Church still observes some elements of the Jewish Law. But on the whole the way things turned out confirms my own (admittedly controversial) account of Jesus' original message. He taught and in his own person *was*, according to his followers, the end of the Law: the end therefore of the whole era of mediated religion, and the arrival of a new kind of human being in whom religion has completed its historic mission. This new human being, the "Last Man," is a fully unified and complete human being who lives in a new divine/human way, and with unprecedented freedom.

Christian reaction to Jesus' message has been as mixed as the earlier Jewish reaction. Conservative Protestantism has usually regarded "The Sermon on the Mount" as being all very well, but much too lofty to be put into practice until the Kingdom Jesus promised has finally arrived. Maybe we'll behave like that in Heaven, but here on earth sinful humanity must continue to be strictly disciplined, and the bourgeois Christian may continue to expect the state to protect his property by force. Catholicism has been less kind: Jesus' characteristic teaching about love was debated in the controversies about "Pure Love" that flared up frequently between the fourteenth and seventeenth centuries, but at the Council of Trent the view of Jesus (genuine love goes altogether beyond, and quite disregards, justice) was condemned in favour of the more Aristotelean view that love rests upon and requires justice. Ideas of self-love and of merit are confirmed: for example, the believer loves God in the entirely-justified expectation of receiving a heavenly reward for doing so. Faith quite rightly expects a payoff, and will get one. Thus mainstream Western Christianity, from its own point of view, has quite rightly condemned Jesus' teaching as heretical, and believers are instead brought up to believe that he taught that "you shall love your neighbour *as yourself*," despite his well-attested criticism of that view. It's easy to love your benefactor, he says, but the real test is whether you can love your *enemy*. To do that requires true greatness of soul, which doesn't resent injustice and fight back against it, but instead rises above it and disregards it. The truly noble person simply does not allow his soul to be poisoned by grievances and grudges: rather, the truly noble person does not even *notice* the wrongs done to him. On this point Jesus is not far from Nietzsche, and someone like Nelson Mandela might have learnt from either—though my guess is that in fact he probably learnt from Jesus via Gandhi. And it is to be noticed that where admirers of Nietzsche might point us to the maxim, "Live dangerously," those who admire Jesus most will prefer to sum *his* view up in the maxim, "Live *generously*."

Jesus' teaching has then seldom been popular with Christians. (Who does one think of? Francis, sundry mystics and heretics, a few important early humanitarians . . .) But he has done much better with Hindus and Buddhists, who have been less confused by the Church's great chain of supernatural doctrines about him. To this day, one is often surprised by how quickly Asians pick out the essential features of Jesus' ethic and express warm admiration.

In conclusion, the ethical teaching of Jesus in Galilee, approximately—and perhaps best—preserved in Q/Luke (i.e., the teaching material common to Matthew and Luke, which in the opinion of many or most scholars is better preserved in Luke's version of it), is Act Four of our new Grand

Narrative theology and completes the main story. The plot is complete: everything has come together and there is only the endless, purely-contingent flow of things in our language-formed human life-world. There's the *humanum* (the concrete universal human) and there is the poignant beauty of transience; nothing else. After Galilee there is no further or greater reality for us to aspire to. We've reached the summit, the very top. I've no idea whether Jesus fully got there personally, but I think he saw and showed what it was, and is.

What has happened since—what humanity has done with this vision of what we could be—will be the topic of a second, subsidiary story which has to explain why the 1980 years since then have on the whole been such a letdown. It will interpret the history of Christianity as repeating the same circular movement, by going out into catholic elaboration, and then returning into immediacy in our own time. For the present, we must review the journey so far. We started by asking how human consciousness and the human world first arose out of the turbulent, chaotic, and largely-inaccessible darkness of animal life in prehuman times. The answer was that the universal term, the Word, the Totem, the kind, moved on the interface between a subject that as yet knew nothing of itself, and a world that was still chaotic. The Word—or better, words in motion—began to classify things, and thereby to make the world intelligible and life liveable. Religion began with that living Word, the moving sign, the Universal term, by which the world of the early hunter-gatherers is ordered.

Imagine that at that very beginning you are the subject of experience. Language moves across the transparent screen of perception, shaping the world, ordering it, lighting it up. In the process, and by an effect I sometimes compare with earthshine, the ordering and illuminating *logos* (or word) on the screen of perception also shines a little light backwards towards *you*, so that you begin to get some primitive idea of your own selfhood. But the only vocabulary that is moving upon that screen is a vocabulary that has been found effective in shaping and ordering the world, a point from which three vital consequences follow:

1. The external world is made *first*, and the self comes second.
2. We have only a borrowed, metaphorical vocabulary for describing the self.
3. We will not be able to ascribe more unity to the self than we currently feel able to ascribe to the world.

By today, with the huge growth of modern Western science, we have been able to build for ourselves a very large and highly differentiated world. Our picture of ourselves so far remains less developed and unified. But what about the third term, namely the world-ordering and energizing power of the Word (the Logos, language)? I have argued that its history effectively coincides for a very long period with the history of religion. The whole supernatural world in effect coincided with culture, which was language in motion. Religion was a way of representing and confirming the power of language to create our world, to create us, and to guide our lives. Religion gave to us all the normative ideas, the ideals and values, by which we oriented our lives and became ourselves.

In Act Two of the Grand Narrative (see chapter 4, above) we briefly recalled the fullest development of Bronze-Age religion in the early religion-based civilizations. Religion became extremely objectified, and both the cosmos and, within it, the state became great hierarchies of sacred power and authority. The whole system was very grand and alluring, to such an extent that we are still half in love with it today. But the societies it created were all slave societies, which in the end became unendurable.

In Act Three (chapter 7) we began the story of the long struggle against religious alienation by telling of the rise of the individual: the sage, the philosopher and the prophet. These free individuals seek a cosmology and an ethic that are less localist and power-dominated, and more rational. The prophets in particular imagine that the religious problem of the Iron Age might be solved if God himself were to leave his throne in Heaven, abandon the whole system of mediated religion, and take up his residence within the individual human heart. Then people would be able to live the divine life spontaneously. They would have it all **by heart**.

In Act Four, the present chapter, we described the Galilean ethical teaching of Jesus as announcing the fulfilment of the prophetic hope, in a radicalized version. There are various strands in Jesus' ethical teaching, and the one that I particularly fasten upon is "solar," expressivist, and dominated by imagery of radiant light. Burn, shine, put on a good show! There are also other strands that it is hard to eliminate from the tradition. Occasionally Jesus *does* seem to commend a spirituality of "hidden inwardness" or "interiorization," but it is so inconsistent with his solar expressivism that I must set it aside. The self is transient: it burns, and burns out. Everything pours out and passes away, and we should be content to do the same, loving life while we have it. Other critics point to the various sayings of Jesus (even in the earliest layer of Q) that seem to prophesy an early and violent irruption of God into history. I have attempted elsewhere to demythologize such sayings, but if that reply fails then I shall be forced to say that, if taken (sort-of) literally, they are of very poor quality and of no intellectual interest, so that I am as much justified in disregarding them here as physicists are justified in disregarding the equally uninteresting apocalyptic obsessions of Sir Isaac Newton.

So I stick with the theme of a complete return of the entire religious realm into the individual human being, and the opening therefore of a new divine humanity. Of this new humanity, Jesus is the "firstborn," but he is only the first of many. He has no special metaphysical status, because there is no metaphysical order.

Remember, in this context, our general non-realism in philosophy. There is no ready-made Real World, out there and fully independent of our language. There is only the historical succession of world-views, and of understandings of human nature, within the ceaseless motion of our language. In effect, world history coincides with the history of ideas—though this doctrine, first adumbrated by Hegel, must now be stated in a thoroughly linguistic form. Within that frame, I have been presenting my main thesis, which has been and is that it is through the history of religious thought that we have very slowly struggled out of our background in darkness and chaos, and have become ourselves. So, in a certain sense, we made God, and then God made us, completing his work by dying into us. Religious thought has been a laborious business, but it has somehow brought us a very long way. We are only a lot of dumb apes who have somehow been able to dream strange dreams that have lifted us out of the relative darkness of animal life, and have made it at last possible for us moderns to say a whole-hearted Amen to our world, and to our own lives in it.

9

SECOND TIME AROUND

K ant says that there are three great questions of life: *What can I know?*, *What ought I to do?*, and *What may I hope?*[17] Although we do not know at all what he was like as a person, and cannot say how far he was the living embodiment of his own teaching, it does seem that for a while in Galilee Jesus touched the very top, reaching the point at which all three of Kant's questions disappear. The supernatural world and the human lifeworld came together, present and future came together, and everything coalesced into the burning, outpouring ethical *Now*. There's nothing at all but our human angle upon the human lifeworld. Just for now, all things are ours, and there is nothing with the right or the power to challenge our valuations. "Nothing," you may say, "except death and nothingness"? No, not even that. We should experience the transience of life as Grace, and its poignant beauty as Glory. We should live as generously as possible, without any *ressentiment* or ill-feeling at all. And notice that Jesus does *not* associate religion with introversion; that is, with a retreat into one's own inwardness, there to care for one's own immortal soul. No, not that, because for him religion is *extravertive*: it forgets the self and goes out into expression as burning love for life and for the neighbour.

Once we understand Jesus' core message, we understand how for him everything comes circling round, back into its origins in the flow of everyday life and ordinary language, and (as Wittgenstein explains very well) the Great Questions simply disappear.[18] We cease to demand any kind of cosmic attention, or recognition, or reward, or even future. All this, just now, is enough for us. We are content simply to affirm life and love now, without demanding any supplement or correction. And we should certainly not wish to see anyone else brought low. Nor should we even *think* about life after death.

In contemporary language, the kingdom of God had come, and was there for anyone who chose it. Walk in!

An interesting but seldom-remarked feature of Jesus' religion as I have described it is that it is not irrational. A very marked feature of church-religions, so called "creeds," is that they require every believer to hold many beliefs for which there is no good evidence, and many more that are obviously untrue. But Jesus' religion is simply a call to ethical decision. It asks us to commit ourselves wholeheartedly to burning love for life and for our fellow-humans. It does tell us to disregard anxiety, persecution and the like. But it is, in the jargon, "non-cognitive." It does not actually require us to hold any supernatural beliefs at all. It certainly does not offer us promises of life after death in another world in exchange for obedience to authority in this life. There should surely be a few human beings who will be interested in a religion that is true—or, at the very least, not obviously untrue.

So what went wrong? Nietzsche says that there has been only one Christian, and he died upon a cross; which means, I think, that Jesus' horrible and tragic death caused a loss of nerve. The fullness of the ethical vision was soon forgotten. Instead, the very small surviving group concentrated their attention upon trying to understand the religious meaning of what had happened. To guide them, they had the Hebrew Scriptures and other related materials provided by their own culture, and they had their own traditions about the Lord's sayings and their own fast-fading recollections of him. Something of their debates survives in the complex many-layered Passion Narratives preserved in the Gospels. Those narratives aren't historical; they are records of the early debates about what, as they thought, must have happened. Not what *did* happen, but what surely *must* have happened.

During the 40s they gradually came to believe that Jesus was not simply and finally lost. No, he had been exalted to Heaven, there to wait as Messiah-designate. Before long he would return in glory to establish his Kingdom on earth for ever. This expectation was to remain strong for several decades.

Meanwhile, the community needed to remain in existence, organized and vigilant, awaiting his return. It needed leaders, and indeed the chief interest at stake in all the early doctrinal debates was the leadership—contested, probably, between James, Peter, and (latterly) the newcomer Paul.

The emergent leadership (all males: Mary Magdalene was not even considered, even though she was widely agreed to be the first witness) derived their authority from the vindicated Jesus. They claimed to have been commissioned by the Lord to be witnesses to his resurrection; and in time it was further claimed that their special authority as teachers of the true faith was transmitted down the line of their successors in office.

Thus by the year 50 or so the Church was already emerging as a multinational society and a new credal religion, "the Way" or, as it eventually came to be called, "Christianity."[19] The old Bronze-Age cosmology, with a heavenly world above and a long chain of command rising above your head all the way up to the highest heaven—all that was coming back. The focus of attention had already been shifted from fulfilment to vigilant expectation, and from Jesus' teaching to his person—and in particular to his exalted status in the cosmic hierarchy. Above all, the apostles had already seized full control of the Church. They and they alone determined true doctrine. "Christianity" is the product of a clerical power-struggle, and that remains its chief interest. Jesus, well ahead of his time, had wanted his hearers to choose a new kind of divine/human life in a new world. But within twenty years of his death he had been made the basis for a relaunch of the old Bronze-Age type of religion—a religion of spiritual power that most of us are still stuck with today. Jesus had promised final fulfil-ment, the very top, right *now*, if we will but choose it. But "Ur-Catholicism," the new religion, postponed eternal hap-piness into the far future—which, for most, would turn out to be an imaginary heavenly world after death. Meanwhile, you must live like a serf, keeping your head down, working hard, believing exactly what you were told to believe and keeping the Church's law, on pain of very severe punish-ment.

It took about 350 years for the whole system to become fully developed. In the first generations total numbers long remained surprisingly small. During the second century we begin to hear of local (but certainly not yet of universal) versions of the *New Testament canon*, of local *baptismal creeds*, and of local *liturgies*. During the early third century more is heard of local *disciplinary canons*, too. But the struggle to develop, agree and enforce canonical forms only gets going in a big way during the fourth century. The period during which it was rather frightening to be baptized, because the sacrament put you for life under the juridical authority of a persecuting Church that might burn you to death for her-esy, lasted from about 400–1700 CE.

There is a wide gulf between the teaching I have as-cribed to the original Jesus, and the developed religious system that later claimed to have been founded and com-missioned by him. Jesus had taught that the Summum Bonum, life's final goal, was all-out solar living and solar loving, right now. What we got was absolute monarchy, and therefore absolute serfdom, both in heaven and on Earth. A landowner's religion, an ideology of law and power that saw the entire Universe organized like an army, with its chain of command rising up above your head all the way up to the Prime Mover and First Cause of everything.

Why is the contrast not more obvious to people? I suggest that there never was a period of primitive Christian purity. On the contrary, the development towards early Catholicism starts in the so-called "tunnel period" immediately after Jesus' death. Catholicism's supernaturalist world-view and philosophy of history is *already* presupposed by the first use of the title "Christ," and the gradual emergence of the belief in Jesus' exaltation to Heaven; and Catholicism's interest in clerical power and accreditation is already present in the leadership contest between James, Peter and Paul. Who was first into the Empty Tomb, whom did the Lord personally commission, who is the best-accredited teacher and ruler of the Church? It comes as no great surprise that the majority-opinion in the New Testament is Peter, Peter, Peter.

But more than that, the conflict between the original outlook of Jesus himself and the remodelled Jesus of the emergent Church is *already* deeply embedded within the best texts we have, making it very difficult in all periods for people to hear Jesus' own voice.

Take, for example, the core of the "Sermon on the Mount," long regarded by most readers of the New Testament as the principal source for Jesus' own teaching, and see the way in which the two outlooks are interwoven in the long passage, Matthew 5:11–6:34.

First, mark with a highlighter passages that witness to a conservative religious outlook that takes for granted the value of a strictly-interpreted religious Law, and a piety of secret good works and hidden inwardness which pursues and expects a heavenly reward after death. That rather secretive and repressed religion is found in 5:17–33, and 6:1–20 and 24.

Next, with a different-coloured highlighter mark passages that witness to a very different, almost existentialist, ethic of open whole-hearted expression, and freedom from anxiety or calculation. This very extravertive religion of putting on a good performance is taught in 5:13–16, 38–48, and 6:25–34.

The difference is astonishing. In the two groups of sayings we find two entirely different, indeed *opposite* religious personalities. Enough, I think, to show the need for much more sophisticated *theological*, and indeed *philosophical*, criticism of the primary sources that we have had so far. The dominant styles of biblical criticism for almost two centuries have been purely historical, source-critical, and literary; and frankly, they have made little or no religious impact upon the public because they have entirely missed what is most important in the texts.

Now we see why our main Grand Narrative had to end where it did, with Jesus' preaching in Galilee. That was the top, the very top. Try it: it's yours. After that there is, in several senses, nothing left to be said. As for the dream of absolute knowledge that lasted from Parmenides to Hegel (from about -500 to +1800 CE), we should forget it. Even Church Christianity had built into it the recognition that as the seraphs outrank the cherubim, so love is higher than knowledge. Even Church-Christianity has got *some* things right. But what's the meaning of the almost-immediate lapse into Ur-Catholicism? It seems that we are starting out upon a second great circle. The first great circle, in Acts One to Four of the Grand Narrative, took us down from primitive immediacy at the dawn of humanity, out into the maximum degree of religious hierarchization and objectification in Bronze Age religion, and then back via the critical individual (sage, philosopher or prophet) into

Jesus' vision of how we should relate ourselves to life in a regained immediacy. Now we seem to be off again, back into the Bronze Age, back to a great pyramid of sacred power both in Heaven and on earth, back into intellectual serfdom and heavily postdated salvation. It peaked in the Bull *Unam Sanctam* (1300), which gives to the Pope—or rather, in which the Pope seizes for himself—a jurisdiction almost as wide as God's. Then, in the merchant classes and amongst other educated townspeople, we begin to hear the first stirrings of protest and the beginnings of the Church's long decline. Individualism, critical thinking, a longing for emancipation—it all returns.

The double circle here is a matter of great interest. Note that it explains why the West has had *two* periods of Enlightenment. In addition, many thinkers have been attracted by the idea that the history of Western thought has moved in a great circle, out into the maximum degree of objectification, and then returning at last into something like an enhanced or heightened version of its own starting-point—like the man in G. K. Chesterton who sailed round the world, came to a magic land, fell in love with a princess, and found that he had come back to his own wife.

For example, Wittgenstein ruminates that philosophy began in ordinariness, with Socrates feigning ignorance as he questioned over-confident young smart-alecs in the marketplace. Gradually, in rationalist metaphysics, philosophy goes out into the highest degree of objectification, and seems to promise absolute knowledge. Then, finally, in the twentieth century philosophy returns into ordinary language and everyday life. And is glad to be back.

Nietzsche has another circular myth. Over the millennia early human beings gradually, gradually grow in confidence that they can understand themselves and their environment. Eventually, by about the second millennium BCE, figures like Abraham and Odysseus are confident that they can live by their wits—so confident, indeed, that they can quite easily outwit their own gods. Surely, they are ready to become free, fully-adult, and critically-aware modern men?

It didn't quite happen. Unfortunately, humankind lapsed into servitude. Great disciplinary institutions such as the State, the Army, and the Church seized power and have held us down for 3000 wasted years. Only now, when critical thinking has just brought about the Death of God, are we back at the point reached by Abraham and Odysseus, and ready to go forward.[20]

There are many, many more such stories in the history of religions and the byways of philosophy. What is unusual about the story being told in this essay is that the wheel turns twice, and the major Fall-event happens half-way through. In the main Grand Narrative we are told an ultra-simplified story in four stages or Acts, as follows:

One: Primitive immediacy, the hunt, totemism and shamanism.

Two: The Agricultural Revolution: religion in early state society. Sacred monarchy, the law-governed Cosmos.

Three: The rise of the free individual moralist, philosopher and prophet.

Four: Jesus in Galilee. The *Summum Bonum* is accessible here and now, not by knowledge but by a free moral choice of it.

That is, or it should be, the end of the story. Or so one might think. But within the Christian era the wheel turns again, as follows:

Second Circle

One: *The legacy of Jesus. The Fall, back into two-worlds dualism and the government of life by religious Law.*

Two: *Christendom. The Christian Empire from Constantine to the Romanovs.*

Three: The rise of critical thinking and modern humanism. Its gradual triumph after Kant in liberal democratic society, in the scientific method, and in humanitarian ethics.

Four: The complete demythologization and rapid decay of ecclesiastical Christianity, and the rediscovery of Jesus, beginning to happen now.

I have printed the whole Second Circle in italics, by way of making the point that it should not claim to be more than a shadow or afterecho of the first. It repeats the events of the Grand Narrative, mainly because the first circle was too big an event to be assimilated the first time around. The whole cycle was therefore repeated within the history of Christianity. Following Nietzsche, an ordinary person's view of why this had to be so might declare that Jesus himself had been much too young, too passionately idealistic, and much too far ahead of his own time. His sudden violent death left his little band confused and leaderless. But in any religious group a leadership vacuum invariably proves irresistibly attractive to power-hungry middle-aged men. They seized power successfully: indeed they did, and they still hold it. But in the process they turned the infant faith into a relaunch of the old Bronze-Age type of religion. To make their new faith seem rational and therefore marketable to the Greeks, it was intellectually reinforced with philosophy to keep it firmly monotheistic. Adopted by Rome in the fourth century CE, the Church's religion became an effective, and very durable political ideology, which in its Austrian, German and Russian versions survived nearly intact until the First World War. Its very similar Islamic version also survived in Istanbul until the same date, and there are still great numbers of young Muslims who long to see the Caliphate restored. Interestingly, they *like* to live under the rule of religious Law, and seem not to imagine an era when it will end—except perhaps in Paradise.

It seems that Islam is still the purest form of theism around. Christianity is rather different: It says that you can choose a different world. It is (or is becoming) a form of nihilistic humanism.

10

COMPLETING THE SECOND CIRCLE

Christian conservatives tend to idealize the period when the Western church was at its grandest and most powerful. The bigger the Church, the better Christianity is doing, they think. They are wrong, because objectified, elaborated religion is always highly disciplinary. Agricultural civilization is always keen on law and order. The worker must accept a setup in which time, space, and his own labour, are all carefully regulated. The cosmos is seen as a larger version of the state that it validates, and both are monarchies. Often the Sun-God rules the cosmos, and the Pharaoh or Inca is his representative on earth. God is the Great Father in Heaven, and the Tsar of All the Russias is the "Little Father" on Earth. God and the *kalifa* (his deputy, in Arabic), Shang and the Emperor of China, the Cosmic Christ and the Christian Roman Emperor . . . the system is so strong that it can co-opt almost *any* religious system and make it serve its purposes. Each monarchy, in each holy city, claims its own personal hotline to the Supreme Being. The social order always tracks the perceived natural order.

The system is always, at least in a broad sense, anti-intellectual. It wants *sobornost*, consent and conformity, and not free thinking, for which it uses words like "heresy." So in Latin Europe as Christendom took shape the great tradition of ancient philosophy and enlightenment died after

almost a thousand years, and the laity slowly sank into il-
literacy. For a while, even kings were illiterate.

It is often thought that the splendour of the art they
produced is a good reason for taking the great world religions in their mediaeval period seriously, and for learning
all about them. Some people even suggest that the splendour of its art is some kind of a reason for thinking Latin
Christian theology could even be *true*. It is not: the reason
why the older church architecture, painting, and music
were so splendid is more likely to have been that it was
only in the field of art that people had any real freedom of
creative religious expression.

An extreme case is Russia, where the Emperor Vladimir
in Kiev accepted Orthodox Christianity from Byzantium
in 988. The Emperor in effect bought a complex religious
system, readymade and unalterable. The Russians found
that they could make space for a contribution of their own
only in the fields of architecture, music, icon-painting,
and (to some extent) personal piety; and so they did. But
intellectually the Church was and has remained stifling.
During the nineteenth century the arrival of the European
Enlightenment and of German Romanticism and Idealism
at last began to wake the Russians up, and a good deal of
lay religious thought developed, but the clergy have remained rigidly conservative and the *Journal of the Moscow
Patriarchate* publishes only historical theology to this day. It
takes the standard Orthodox view that the development of
the Church was completed by the year 787, so that creative
theology stopped then, and will never again be needed.
As for Russian Orthodox *art*, it very early began to have a
rather sad, yearning, nostalgic and *entombed* air, and since
the eighteenth century it has declined steadily into sentimental kitsch. Today, it is "heritage" — that is, dead, dead,
dead.

Once we have digested that example, we can recognize
that the Western story is not so very different, for indeed

today Western church Christianity is rapidly going the same way as Eastern—i.e., losing whatever intellectual content it once had and therefore becoming fossilized, sentimental and kitschy. Between D. F. Strauss and Rudolf Bultmann academic theology made a half-hearted attempt to become critical, but the churches have made it all too clear that they will never be able to reconcile themselves to the critical way of thinking, and today theology is mostly historical only, and makes no difference at all. At the time of the Protestant Reformation, theology for a century and a half became a subject of urgent interest and importance to the people at large, with several dozen interesting and lively new denominations and movements; but today Protestantism has completely lost its old intellectual diversity and vitality, and instead every remaining denomination is largely dominated by the same bland one-size-fits-all Conservative Evangelicalism, a tradition from which no religious writing of merit can ever appear.

At present, only two traditions within Christianity have any strength left, namely the Roman Catholic and the Evangelical Protestant. But neither of them can now tolerate critical thinking, nor even art, and both are intellectually spent. Church Christianity stands very much where the remains of the ancient Bronze-Age city religions stood in the first and second centuries of our era: the temples still stand, and their priests more or less function, but they are becoming a bit of a joke. They provide a little picturesque background for certain major funerals and some other state occasions, but that's about all that can be said for them. As for the theology faculties, the unbelieving theologian has been a feature of the Western campus at least since Franz Overbeck (1837–1905). In the days of 1960s "radical theology" he was often a rather troubled figure, and indeed a very reluctant unbeliever like the late Van Harvey; but firmly post-ecclesiastical theologians are now very common, and in due time they will doubtless become the norm.

All this indicates that we are now completing the third act of the second cycle of our Grand Narrative, the period in which charismatic individuals—philosophers, prophets— criticize the current state of religion. Whether in the Bronze Age or in the later Mediaeval period, this is religion at its biggest, grandest and most objectified. It links the state to the cosmos, and its own liturgical year to the agricultural year. It validates the social order, and adds picturesque beauty to the toiling labourer's life. Its monuments and its music, its art, its rituals and its professional clergy are all very grand. But from the point of view of the talented individual it is stifling. It is all a great cultural fiction that is passed off as being cosmic fact and therefore unalterable. It does a great job in keeping the gods and the king on their respective thrones. The priests and the aristocracy are doing very well, too. But the whole system is very traditionalist: it always tends to resist new knowledge and social change, and it fiercely persecutes both the mystics who try to bypass the apparatus of religious mediation and find a short way to Heaven, and the social visionaries who imagine ways of remaking the world and the social order. So in Europe since the fourteenth century the prophets and mystics, and more recently the philosophers, poets and other writers, have been rebels, slowly pushing Church Christianity back into the past. Critical thinking, science-based industry and rapid social change are leaving the Church stranded in a world it can no longer understand.

In modern Europe one sees the best religious thought leaving the old orthodoxy, leaving the churches, and beginning to strike out on its own around the time of the French Revolution and Romanticism, and in the thought of Kant, Hegel, the Young Hegelians (especially Strauss and Feuerbach) and Kierkegaard. More recently, as we approach the twentieth century one begins to realize that the important and interesting religious thinkers are no longer church-oriented clergymen, and no longer members of university

Faculties of Theology. They are more likely to be troubled laypeople, religious existentialists, representative figures of their own nationality and period: people like Unamuno, Dostoyevsky, Simone Weil and Kazantzakis. American agnostics and troubled believers perhaps include Wallace Stevens and John Updike. Interestingly, Islam nowadays produces similar figures: Mahfouz, Said, Pamuk, Rushdie perhaps? There are one or two such figures in Judaism too, starting with Kafka and perhaps Levinas. In addition, it is worth recalling that the greatest modern philosophers all confess to being at least *temperamentally* religious: one thinks of Heidegger, Wittgenstein and Derrida.

Throughout the entire twentieth century people were troubled with thoughts, not only of the crisis of faith, but also of nihilism, the decline of the West, and approaching catastrophe. From Nietzsche to Oswald Spengler, and on to Baudrillard: but where is the new Christ?

As everyone knows, Nietzsche wrote *Also Sprache Zarathustra* as a replacement for the New Testament, and seriously wondered if he was himself the new Christ. In philosophy, he is nearly right. But in his values he is not right. He is a bit too social Darwinist in his scorn for pity, and his celebration of the values of strife, struggle, self-discipline and heroic masculinity. Maybe he's the new Baptist, and maybe no new Jesus is needed. A return of the old one, rediscovered at last, might be best.

11

RELIGIOUS THOUGHT AND
THE MAKING OF MANKIND

Although it makes some use of older materials, the
Hebrew Bible is nowadays increasingly thought to be
a very late compilation, written and arranged in its present
form only three centuries or so before Christ.[21] If it were
historical, we'd have the coins of great kings like David and
Solomon, but we don't; and if Judaism were an ancient religion there would be much more archaeological evidence for
Yahwism (the worship of Yahweh/"Jehovah") at least in the
form of theophoric names, just as in our own society many
Muslims bear names that are clear evidence of their religion. But early evidence (pre-300 BCE) of ancient Yahwism
is either sparse or entirely lacking, and even conservative
scholars are increasingly inclined to admit that the Hebrew
Bible as a book is much more like Sir Thomas Malory's
Morte d'Arthur than it is like the *Anglo-Saxon Chronicle*.
The Hebrew Bible is not a record of historical events, but a
national myth and an admonitory epic about an ideal past,
written many centuries or even millennia after the events it
purports to describe. Frankly, the past is a human creation.

Given that the Bible has this general character, it is
hardly surprising that in Genesis ancient Israel projects its
own national god back to the beginnings of human existence, and even into the first creation of the world out of
the primal chaos. Although one or two people were still

defending the idea of "primitive monotheism" as late as the twentieth century, no scholar today supposes that monotheistic religion can be traced back into Palaeolithic times. Nowadays we look at cave paintings and at the way of life of the early hunters, and suppose that the earliest forms of religion were surely shamanistic, and had to do especially with mankind's relations with animals. In my new Grand Narrative I suggested, accordingly, that for our purposes we should widen the use of the word "god" to include the complex early pictures of the supernatural realm that only gradually became condensed and unified into standard monotheism. Like the USA, God himself is, historically at least, *E pluribus unum*. The Hebrew Bible itself preserves several divine Names, one of which—Elohim—is plural.

When all this has been said, it nevertheless remains true that the Hebrew Bible is an extraordinarily memorable book. I know no other that has so gripped and held my imagination. Why? Some people have been suggesting recently that the chief fascination is with the personality that it ascribes to God—a huge, impossibly-demanding, volatile, capricious, implacable, inescapable male child with only a low level of self-awareness; as if God personifies pure, domineering, difficult, primitive maleness. The point is well taken, as the phrase goes, but it puts all the emphasis upon what God demands of human beings, and the kind of overbearing personality they see him as having.[22] To me the prior and much bigger topic is the way in which God always leads, and does everything first. He acts as a scout or vanguard, going ahead and working everything out so that we can follow behind him and occupy the territory that he has opened up for us. God showed us how to be selves who have a world and can act in it.

Thus it is God who in the beginning finds himself confronted by pure chaos and darkness.[23] He hasn't yet got a world, so he hasn't yet got a self, a subjectivity, either. He's

in the dark, as the phrase goes. How's he to make a move and become something? He has to go out of himself by a founding act of expressive freedom, and divide up this darkness into the great cosmic zones. He must sort the foaming restless chaos out into general kinds, each with its own name. He must *describe* a world, he must *form* his world by using language. Hence his first great cry, *Fiat lux*, Let there be light!, which is both a linguistic utterance, a one-word sentence, and itself a lightning bolt that illuminates the endless watery waste. In this way God's very first speech draws the line between light and darkness, language and non-language, and begins to make him conscious of himself as a subject who has a world, a speaker whose uttered words have formed and made beautiful the chaos and darkness of pre-linguistic consciousness.

Notice that so far the chaotic watery waste of darkness and non-language, the Wholly Other, has not yet been *finally* conquered. It is under control, and in its place, but by no means dead yet. God has plenty more to say, and where there is more to be said nothing is yet finally fixed.

As God speaks on, the cosmos becomes divided into regions, structured in space and time, and populated with a variety of beings. It becomes brighter, more focussed. God becomes more vividly aware of himself as having a world that is unified, ordered, present to him, and a theatre in which, as a speaker and agent, he can act to achieve a purpose. God now has a *stage*.

What next? God creates the first man in two sexes, male and female, in his own image and speaking like him. Man is God's finite counterpart and the agent through whom his purpose is to be fulfilled. These two humans are given the power of procreation, so that they can create for themselves offspring, descendants and a social world. God further delegates his own powers to them by giving them rule over the animal and plant kingdoms. In another version of the creation myth God gives to the man the work of naming the animals, even before the creation of woman. It is the man, after all, who is to be the hunter. He really needs power over animals.

In the whole story so far God shows that everything he has done has been done in order to be a lesson to us, and with the object of handing over to us. From God we are to learn how we ourselves, each one of us, must find the strength and courage to face up to the foaming chaos of raw experience, and speak. Just through our own human conversation we must find the strength to posit, to classify, to order, to illuminate, to unify and to *appropriate* our world; and as we do so, we slowly become ourselves, as beings who have a world that we can at least begin to order and control, a world in which we can act to achieve our purposes.

Let us return here to the dark foaming chaos, a few tens of thousands of years ago, in which it all began. At that stage of our existence we were barely conscious of ourselves as subjects. Shut your eyes again, take your time, and check. The chaos is so formless that I am not aware of myself as a complex self. There isn't enough backlight being reflected off the world to light up my self. I'm not even aware of myself as a subject. All that can be said is that "there is awareness of this featureless sparkling darkness." That's very little.

How is progress to be made? We noted earlier that in front of the foam there may be a few greenish-yellow floating shapes, after-images of the window or of the lightbulb that you were looking at a few moments previously. At least it can be said that regular shapes may drift across or hang in front of the chaos. Also there are moments when the chaos does become more focussed and concentrated. The scene lights up a little: there is concentration upon flint-knapping, or upon the hunt, or upon social grooming, or sex. These episodes don't yet connect together enough to establish a continuous and self-aware subject, by any means: but there is in them the beginning of consciousness and of sociability.

Much more intense—and this is something we still feel vividly—is the fierce stab, or lightning bolt, of illumination when we suddenly hear a sharp cry of warning or command. There is a kind of jactation. We are jolted into acute consciousness, and time slows. Have you ever noticed that we always think of the Creator's first utterance as a sharp cry of just that kind? It's an electrifying shout of command, and one is violently jolted wide awake by it. That's our feeling about the beginning of language, and the power of language. Lucretius (who was very acute, for a Roman) was well aware of this point.

There are other factors in the rise of language. There is for example the use of melodies and other musical codes to co-ordinate worksongs, to communicate over great distances, to induce trance, and to stir men's martial feelings. The social uses of music as a form of language are both very ancient indeed, and still as lively as ever: listen to the bugle, the pipes, the drums, the organ. Equally important is the babbling and the cuchi-cooing that leads to the development of speech in babies. One may say that phatic sounds of many kinds preceded and led smoothly into the use of all our fully-developed natural languages. And one should probably add in here, as precursors of language that are still in use today, the very wide range of gestures, signals and "body-language" that still survives everywhere, and especially amongst hunters and soldiers who must communicate silently.

So we should see language as developing slowly and continuously over a very long period. As it develops, it produces first an increasingly well lit-up and unified world, and secondly, an increasingly well-lit and unified subjectivity, as we begin to get ourselves together.

However, our knowledge of ourselves has developed only very slowly, and with much difficulty. Even before we got much of a view of ourselves, we were already rapidly developing our ideas about another realm that is also both very ancient and very up-to-date. The world of signs, or the world of language, hangs *between* the slowly emerging conscious human self *and* the foaming darkness of raw experience, the white noise (or "the manifold of intuition," as Kant calls it). On that floating screen before our eyes move the words, the signs, the shapes, the patterns through which we see the foaming darkness, and are able to make a world out of it. The most important and ancient of these signs that hang before our eyes and help us to interpret our experience are general terms or kinds like *bear!* or *gazelle!* It was vital to the survival of early humans that they got these general signs before their eyes and stayed firmly focussed upon them, so that when they went out hunting together, they quickly got locked on to the relevant animal when it turned up, and *collectively* responded to it in the appropriate manner. Our new Grand Narrative starts from the idea that religion was originally necessary to our survival. The earliest humans had big brains, but didn't know what to do with them. They needed powerful general symbols of the most important features of their environment, and they needed a strict and repetitive discipline to fix their communal attention upon those symbols. So that world of signs or symbols that hangs between the mind and raw experience is the world of religion. Religion impresses it upon us. With its help we can build a world and survive. It also helps us to understand itself—and, eventually, our own selves, too.

This enigmatic, hard-to-see world that hangs always before my eyes, and that helps me make sense of everything—what's its status, what shall we call it? Philosophy calls it the world of intelligible *Forms*, says Plato. No, it's just a world of *concepts*, says Aristotle. On the contrary, they are just *words*, says mediaeval Nominalism. It's the *transcen-*

dental a priori, says Kant, who invented an extremely clever way of analyzing it. It's the world of *Geist*, says Hegel. It's the world of our *ideal culture*, says anthropology after Durkheim. It's the world of *language*, says Wittgenstein. It's the world of signs in motion, says modern French philosophy. It's my *culture*, it's *tradition*, it's my *identity*, say ordinary people nowadays.

In one way and another, the philosophers have managed to invent a good deal of baffling terminology and to muddy the waters pretty thoroughly. But there's worse to come. What does religion call this same world?

It's *the Dreaming*, populated by mythic beings, say the Australians (the aboriginal ones, that is). It's the *spirit-world* through which the Shaman journeys in his trance, say the Inuit. It's the ancient *supernatural* world of the mythic past: "in those days." It's the *abode of the dead*, the underworld: haven't you noticed how the dead somehow manage to look down benignly upon you all the time from a place where they are enthroned inside your head? They are still watching over you, passing on their wisdom, making sure you remain faithful to Tradition. No, say others, it's better to say that the invisible world you live by is *the heavenly world*, full of angels; or that it's the *Divine Mind*, which contains all the universal divine Ideas, the patterns that God held before *his* mind while he was making everything. The Holy Spirit links God's Mind to your mind, illuminating you and leading you into all truth. All understanding and all truth depend upon this participation of the human mind in the Eternal Divine Mind—or so says Christian Platonism. Yes, the Platonist really thinks that the set of ideas that hangs between your mind and chaos exactly parallels the set of ideas that God has in his mind. You really are a chip off a very big Old Block.

Now there is more: What are the objects, or the beings, that populate this unseen world through which we see everything?

Religion says they are *totems*, they are ancestral *animal spirits*, they are Egyptian-style *gods with animal heads*, they are the *angels*, divine messengers (angel is Greek for messenger), they are the *Divine Ideas*, they are what we might today call *religious symbols.*

Why these complications? In the West philosophy began as a critique of religion. It did not like the way religion always wants to reify, personify, and tell stories about the terms we must use in order to make sense of our experience. So philosophy and religion separated into two distinct—or supposedly distinct—traditions. The two traditions have often tried to keep apart. But they have equally often noticed that they are developing along parallel lines, and have got themselves tangled up together again. Hence Christian Platonism, and hence also the kind of "radical theology" I do, which is steeped in German Idealist philosophy (Kant and Hegel) and modern French "theory." By now, the terminology has become too scrambled and confusing for non-specialists to cope with—perhaps for *anyone* to cope with. I apologize for having had to employ a lot of difficult terminology. Yet the basic thesis that I am using for my Grand Narrative is quite simple: the world of religion is the world in our heads, transcendent*al*, and not transcen-dent,[24] the large body of cultural programming that has enabled us to build a world and to survive. Religion and the typically religious kind of thinking and acting developed this programming and impressed it upon us. Eventually religion gradually made us better at understanding itself, and indeed our own selves, too. And, to end this section of the argument with a oneliner: God created us; which, being demythologized, means that religion created us. It dragged us out of wild nature, disciplined us, and made us everything we are. Our heads are still full of it, more full than most of us recognize.

Now we continue the story, by briefly thinking about how God in the Hebrew Bible invents civilization—the topic of Act Two of the main new Grand Narrative. The old nomads flitted over their ancestral lands, but made little permanent impression upon the soil. Because they had not yet **put down roots** in any one particular place, their theology, their world-view, their religion and their selfhood were not yet *centred* and hierarchized. They were still relatively democratic, because a nomadic society of hunter-gatherers is not yet truly a *class* society, nor a *caste* society. But when God settles in his own House, in the middle of his own holy City, in the middle of his own Holy Land, he establishes a clear and intelligible system of degrees of holiness as a fact, on the ground. It is like a butt, an archery target on which are marked a series of concentric circles. The highest value is concentrated in the bull's eye at the Centre, and as you move away from the centre the degree of concentrated sacred power falls gradually (which means "step-by-step").

When the god settles in one place, he creates on the ground a fixed central focus of the Sacred, with a series of concentric rings around it that runs out to the frontiers of his domain. Nor is this the only system of gradations that he establishes: there is a vertical line, the *axis mundi*, that runs down from the highest Heaven above to the god's throne where he sits on his holy mount, and then on down to the lowest pit of the underworld. The whole cosmos is liable to be seen as a system of concentric spheres, as in Dante's *Divine Comedy*. It rotates slowly upon its axis, like a gyroscope. And, in addition, there is a social hierarchy that is more-or-less linked with your address, because the top people always live closest to the Centre: the King, the Court, the military, the merchants and craftsmen within the City walls, the peasant farmers in the fields, and (at the bottom) the itinerant day-labourers. All these look towards the Central focus of holiness, power, justice, and exchange. To this day we remain imbued with that old model to an astonishing degree, and we are still passing it on virtually intact to each new generation. It is deeply theological. To this day the philosopher, or prophet, or cultural radical who wants to persuade us that our 5,000-year-old standard-model religious cosmology is now an incubus, something we really need to throw off permanently—to this day anyone who bears such a message can be sure of being given a hard time.

With good reason. The old model created us, it made all of us what we are. We owe everything to it. That is why we remain so religious. Even the most able and original of us has not given the old world-view up without some reluctance and pain. One might say that the history of Western thought since about the time of Erasmus, Luther and Copernicus has been the history of the long struggle to free ourselves from the old ways of thinking. Repeatedly, revolutionaries have believed themselves entitled to claim success: the French Revolution, Nietzsche and the Death of God, the Russian Revolution. But each time the claim has turned out to be a little premature. In a somewhat weakened form, the old system of thought has come back repeatedly, and the promised New Man has had to be postponed. All of us are still at least fifty per cent Old Men.

This time, however, things will turn out differently. Won't they?

12

THE TWILIGHT OF THE GODS

The old Western Grand Narrative, begun in the Bible, slowly grew until it was definitively stated by Augustine in his *The City of God* (413–26), but (arguably) didn't reach its late peak—its Viceroy's Palace moment[25]—until Calvin's *Institutes of the Christian Religion* (1536). By the time of Milton's *Paradise Lost* (1667), its collapse was inevitable. Half a lifetime earlier, Milton had met the aged Galileo: he could not fail to know what was happening.

The old Western Christian cosmology has a simpler history. It was slowly assembled from various sources, including the Bible, Claudius Ptolemy's *Almagest* (2nd century CE: Ptolemy's cosmology was also adopted by the Muslim Arabs), and the Pseudo-Dionysius (usually *The Celestial Hierarchy*, c. 500 CE). But it peaked, and received one supreme literary expression, in Dante's *Divine Comedy* (c. 1302–1312 CE). For the next two-and-a-half centuries it was clearly presupposed by the great Italian painters, and is especially vivid in Fra Angelico and in Botticelli's drawings. After Copernicus it rapidly declined, as the new heliocentric "system of the world" prevailed. Milton still presumes it, but with conscious reservations.

The long twilight of the gods—that is, the decay and final collapse of the old Grand Narrative and its associated cosmology—has been going on in the West, as we can now see, for almost 500 years. Its life has been, to some extent, artificially prolonged by the hymns, the liturgy and the power interests of the churches: otherwise, we'd be hard put to it to explain why so many people still believe in angels, or why a prominent nineteenth-century hymnodist is so sure that "There's a home for little children / Above the bright blue sky." Did she herself really think that—or was she merely using an idiom that she somehow felt was expected of her? It's hard to say, but C. S. Lewis, who held a Cambridge Chair in Mediaeval and Renaissance Literature, made a half-hearted attempt to revive the old cosmology as late as the 1950s.[26] Philip Pullman, a contemporary, does not believe in it at all, but still draws upon it and alludes to it in his three-volume children's epic *His Dark Materials* (1995–2000). So unkillable is our nostalgia that after-echoes of "The Sea of Faith('s) . . . melancholy, long, withdrawing roar" are still heard today. The tradition of Anglican poetry lives on, even though the poets themselves are no longer quite believers.[27] As another late-Anglican poet has put it, we cling desperately to our dead gods.

We are so nostalgic that we even clutch at the remains of a faith that we vociferously reject. Richard Dawkins, for example, is preoccupied with a God he no longer believes in. Why? It's a case of "holding on to Nurse / for fear of finding something worse." While he's looking at the God he doesn't believe in, Dawkins can justly feel good: he is superior, rational, relatively liberated. Best of all, he can postpone thinking seriously about what is left to him after God. In the "continental" tradition since Nietzsche, many people have tried hard to think about what's left to us after God is quite gone and forgotten; but in the English-speaking world we have preferred to cling to our more comfortable half-belief and our unbelief. We are in no hurry to find out just how much God will take away with him when he finally vacates his former property.

So what is left to us, after God? Nietzsche says simply: "Nihilism," or, less briefly, "There is no moral world-order"—meaning, no moral providence, no objective endorsement of our moral values. Nothing out there *backs us up*, or confirms either our judgements or our valuations. We really are on our own, contingent beings in an utterly contingent world. Nothing out there ensures either that the world can make sense *to us*, or that *we* can make sense of it.

Since Nietzsche, there is more to say. Philosophy has drifted closer towards the view I call "anthropomonism," the view that all we'll ever know is **our world**. We have no access to an absolute or "perspectiveless" vision of **the world**. All we can ever know, and therefore in effect all that there is, is **our world**, a world already shaped by the language, the cultural programming, the Tradition, that is inside our own heads. Hence my battle to find a way to re-think religion purely from within anthropomonism. That's all we've got, and we'll never have or know anything else. The most I'll allow in the way of objective extra-human reality is roughly what the excellent American philosopher Hilary Putnam allows: in open conversation with others I can help to evolve a common, tested, public vision of the world, a world-view that works (for now) and therefore can reasonably be trusted (for now). It's constantly changing and developing all the time, as everyone knows, but we can't do better than go along (for now) with today's best, human-only, consensus: that is, today's best available story. I call this "human realism." It's a publicly and politically marketable version of my own private position, which is a bit more sceptical. But ordinary journalists, scientists and politicians are quite right to emphasize the need constantly to work away at establishing and maintaining a rational public consensus about our world.

If something like that is our human situation after God, what does it now seem that belief in God was all about? In retrospect, and in the light of our present discussion, it now seems that the rise of settled civilized life and of farming was crucial to the development of monotheism, and of belief in life after death. To take life after death first, ever since, in 1953, the British archaeologist Kathleen Kenyon found plastered skulls on the lowest levels of her excavation at Jericho, it has been generally thought that when human beings first began to take up the settled life of farmers, the dead suddenly became more important than they had been before. Why? Because in the new order your standing in the world depends upon your relationship to your own ancestral property. It's your livelihood, your *patrimony*. Your *title* to it derives from your dead father; and all around the world we begin to notice how important his father's bones now are to a man. His dead father has become part of his own mental furniture, the apparatus through which he relates himself to his world. But that means that his dead father is now part of the world of gods and spirits by which he is guided. He will therefore probably believe now in his father's life after death, as a venerated ancestor "up there" looking benignly down upon him. It will seem natural to keep his father's bones close by him, as reassuring evidence of his own place and his title. In Jericho, the skulls were found under house floors; in other places the bones may be buried at the highest point of the family "portion" of land, or in a specially-built mausoleum or ossuary.

In the new farming culture, patriliny and patrimony became important. Genealogy legitimates, and in many places even the gods have genealogies. Behind Zeus, the living patriarch of the gods, in his distant father Chronos, and behind Chronos is an even remoter figure, *his* father Ouranos. Interestingly, in Bronze Age religion dead gods still "worked," and could still be worshipped. Osiris and Pluto are the best-remembered of them.

So much for life after death, which is mentioned here because I have noticed that when men reach my age they have a tendency to become interested in genealogy. We turn now to the other great preoccupation of the settled human being's life, namely his relation to God. Here we suddenly see that the real issue in debates about what is idiotically called "the existence of God" is the early farmer's need for a strong founding and protective Centre *over there*, of which he can be comfortably aware all the time. At the Centre is the enthroned god, from whom radiates sacred power and authority. Soldiers, or at least weapons, are maintained at the Centre. The market is there, and craftsmen live there. At least once a year, the farmer *goes up* to it to trade and to attend festivals. In fact, his whole life *revolves* around the Centre.

Everywhere, one goes *up* to the Centre, because everywhere the god's seat is thought of as being on high ground. In England we still love walking *up* to our hillforts, which nowadays are understood to have functioned as proto-cities for the people who lived within sight of them, and looked up to them. The ancient Israelite went *up* to God's house in Jerusalem, the *Temple Mount*, just as today the English still go *up* to London, where St Paul's Cathedral is on Ludgate *Hill*, as Cambridge's leading parish church is on Market *Hill*. We do not allow the fact that both London and Cambridge lie low and look flat to worry us: indeed, Cambridgeshire has a hillfort out in the fens (Stonea Camp at TL448930, nr. Wimblington) that is only about 1½ metres above the surrounding waters. No doubt, in its heyday the fenmen still thought of themselves as "going up" to it.[28]

I'm saying that belief in God always involves belief that every complex "organic" whole needs and has a strong founding and directing Centre to hold it together. God at the cosmic level, the monarch at the level of the state, and the rational soul at the level of the individual human being. The same notion gets secular transcriptions in the metaphysics of *substance*, and in recent uses of the word "*identity*." The idea that the gods are always *up* is transcribed into philosophy as the idea that the individuating principle at the Centre that holds everything together is at a "higher" level of being.[29] It is the "core," even the "essence," and is thought of as unchanging.

All this helps to explain why the Death of God is such a great event. God takes away with him all ideas of objective order, intelligibility, permanent reality and value. *Everything* crumbles. Rioters and looters take to the streets. People sense an analogy: after the King dies, how can we ensure the continuity and order of the state?—and after God dies, how are we to rethink and rebuild knowledge, ethics and our own lives?

In the short run, one can always claim that, as in ancient society, the dead God, the dead King, and the dead parent somehow live on in death, and continue to validate and support us in the world that has survived them. But in the long run one knows that the Death of God implies the end of *all* our ideas of a permanent, intelligible reality out there, permanent values, and permanent truths. Everything, really everything is contingent and is passing away. In the short run, a modern person can and does take some comfort from the thought that her genes will go on, for a while; and her descendants will remember her, for a while. But everything is contingent, death is simple extinction, and we haven't got long. We are only our own outsides: there is no permanent core-identity inside us. We are only the burning and burning-out of the process of our own lives, for the next few years. That's all there is, and all we are.

All his has gradually been recognized by us in the West during the long twilight of the gods that has occupied the last four or five centuries. Who were the first to know? Marlowe, Shakespeare, Montaigne, maybe. Certainly Hume. Some at least of the contemporaries of Schopenhauer, such as Franz Schubert. But realization begins to spread really widely only during the later years of the nineteenth century. Nietzsche is the greatest, by some distance. Samuel Beckett is perhaps the most *personally* attractive and eloquent recent figure. But then the message reaches the churches themselves, and after the cultural flare-up of the 1960s their decline accelerates. Today we do at last begin to see that everyone—at least, in Europe—now sort-of knows the score.[30] The old vision of the chief end of human life as being a state of eternal happiness in the secure possession of absolute knowledge of an absolutely perfect One is at last utterly gone. Now there is only the burning, for a short while. We will never know that we have come to the end. That's why there is no full stop at the end of life's sentence

I am suggesting, of course, that we have come to the end of Act Three of the second circle of our new Grand Narrative. The criticism of fully-elaborated Church Christianity by moralists, philosophers and religious prophets has been completed. I am suggesting that there is now nothing for us but solar living and solar loving, in the time we have left. That is why Jesus in Galilee touched the top, the very top, the *Summum Bonum*. There is nothing more than that, and therefore no future for religion except by a rediscovery of the way of living he happened to be the first to discover and teach.

13

THE HIGHEST GOOD

According to a long tradition in both Western philosophy and Western theology, a human being is an animal distinguished by the possession of a rational soul. There are other sorts of soul—animal souls, for example—but in us the core-self is an immaterial substance, a rational soul, and this makes a big difference. The animal soul is the "principle" of an animal's life. It is part of nature, and dies when the animal does. But a rational soul is more than that, because reason transcends nature. Looking up at the sky, people seemed to see a world very different from the sublunary world. They saw a higher, unchanging world of perfectly spherical bodies that moved in regular, predictable courses, a heavenly world, a world with which our reason has a special affinity and a world peculiarly satisfying to contemplate. In short, a better world.

Against this background it seemed natural to most philosophers, all the way through from Plato to the Enlightenment, to hold a dualistic view of the human being. Our bodies belong to the visible world, the world of Nature, and are destined for death. But our souls, being finite rational substances, have an affinity with the unchanging heavenly world above, and are by nature immortal. Following Plato, many of the philosophers maintained that the human soul pre-existed in the heavenly world, and now for a while lives embodied on earth. After death the soul will return to its true and eternal home in the world above.

The theologians held the same view of the soul, but they told a somewhat different story about its life-history: for them each human soul has been specially created by God in order to "fit" and to animate one particular newly-conceived human fetus. Our life is a time of probation, and although we suffer from an initial handicap in that we are born in original sin, a sure way to salvation is provided. After death we are provisionally allocated for salvation or damnation, but for a final verdict we must wait until the Last Judgement. If we are acquitted, then our souls will be reunited with their proper bodies, and thereafter we will enjoy eternal happiness in contemplating and praising God.

Although the philosophers and the theologians thus told slightly-different stories, with the philosophers being if anything rather *more* dualistic, and the theologians giving a little more value to the body and to the social character of life after death, they were in substantial agreement upon one point: the contemplative (or in Greek, "theoretical," i.e., visionary) life is higher than the active life. If they were asked what is the Highest Good, or the *Summum Bonum*, for a human being they would give substantially the same answer: it is eternal happiness in the intellectual intuition of, or in contemplating, eternal unity, necessity and perfection of Being. The theologians called this state the Vision of God, or Beatitude. It's what the catechisms speak of as "knowing and loving God, and enjoying him for ever." It is Man's Chief End. So much for the goal of the religious life. The philosopher's goal was the same: it was *intuitive* (as opposed to discursive) *knowledge*, or it was *absolute knowledge*. Between Plato and Hegel, the life of reason was often seen as a journey up a ladder of degrees of knowledge, towards a blessed state of immediate, total, eternal knowledge at the top, the very top. That was the philosophers' heaven, and it was substantially identical with the heaven, not only of

Christians, but also of many Jews and Muslims—and especially of the mystics.

Today, that ancient conception of the Summum Bonum has died, and died so completely that most people have little memory of it.[31] Yet it was once so powerful that even atheists like Shelley could cling to it. Here he is on the death of Keats, whom he calls "Adonais":

> The soul of Adonais, like a star,
> Beacons from the abode where the Eternal are.

From the 1790s to the 1960s people continued to use words like "immortality" and "eternity"—not least, in poetry—even though it was increasingly obvious that both words were now being used only in a metaphorical way. "Eternity" was really just death, and "immortality" fame. Only in the last thirty years or so have most of us felt able to let it be obvious, even at funerals, that we no longer believe in any sort of life after death.

Meanwhile, over the same period a new conception of the human being has been developing, and it is now more than ready to take over.[32] The place to look for its beginnings is in the philosophy of Arthur Schopenhauer. A human being is best understood as a human *life*, and a human life is best understood not as a substance, but as an outpouring process, a bundle of energies that surges out strongly at first, until after seventy or eighty years it peters out. These energies, or "drives," or "appetites," or "emotions," or even "instincts," are numerous. The most basic of them is simply "the will to live," and many of them come in opposed pairs. Thus, as well as the will to live, we may become aware as we grow older of a growing desire for death, and of the *simultaneous* presence within us of the two impulses. Another familiar and amusing example is that of the person who is very domineering in public life, but reveals a markedly masochistic side in bed.

All our impulses seek gratification, but it may be difficult to obtain in the social world. The pleasure principle is frustrated by the reality principle, to use Freud's jargon. When that happens, we may seek relief in some kind of substitute or symbolic gratification; and in the case of conflicting impulses we may seek an outlet which ingeniously relieves both of them simultaneously.

On this biology-influenced account of the human being, a human life is a process of continuous self-expression. In Schopenhauer's language, we, like the whole world of which we are parts, are (noumenal) Will coming out into Representation. In Freud's language, each of us is a bundle of instinctual drives each seeking its own gratification. A few are straightforwardly gratified, as when I have lunch; others find various forms of socially-approved symbolic gratification. We dress up, we parade ourselves, we gossip, and we act out our various social roles. Sometimes in our behaviour we are trying to get ourselves together by acting in a way that synthesizes conflicting impulses; and sometimes other people can "read" this behaviour as "body-language" of ours, and they gossip maliciously about it to each other.

On this newer view, then, the social world is a kind of theatre in which each of us plays several roles. On life's stage I am my own self-expression, I am the process of my own living. I am the show I put on, I am the contribution I make to the various social games I play in, and what you see is pretty much what there is. I'm an open book, and your reading of me is probably quite as good as my own attempted reading of myself. Maybe better. But what I have no use for is the traditional Western notion that my "real self" is an immortal rational soul tucked away somewhere inside me; an entity that God sees very clearly, and which I daily try to examine for my own good. On the old view, my religious life is my hidden "interior life" into which I withdraw in order to examine my conscience and to pray. Now, to me, that old idea has become completely meaningless, and the old spirituality that was based on that theory of the self is a waste of time. Instead, I now take a thoroughly "theatrical" view of the self, seeing it as an ongoing process of expression and communication with others in the human social world. We are the roles we play. We burn, and burn out.

What, in that case, becomes of the *religious* life? Instead of seeing it as a second, inner life, conducted deep inside our own subjectivity, in which we talk "only to God" (like the members of a certain aristocratic family in Boston, Massachusetts), we should now learn to see our religious life in extravertive, emotive and expressive terms.[33] Because much of religious symbolism is healing and reconciling, the practice of religion ought to help us to resolve our inner conflicts and to get ourselves together, so that we can become more outgoing. We completely abandon the notion that religious practice is a way of self-purification by way of getting ready for the Last Judgement and then a life after death in another world. There is no other world. There is only this life, and religion should be helping us not to become more inhibited but to become *less* so, so that we can be more lively, creative, and straightforwardly loving.

On this newer view then, the Summum Bonum, the Highest Good that there is for us human beings, is solar living and solar loving. It is something active and expressive, a habit of living, something that we must *do*, rather than a passive and purely intellectual state of timeless beatitude that we hope to be *given*. And it is purely this-worldly.

Interestingly, the old "eschatological urgency" of being in a hurry because you think the End is nigh has returned in a new form. You used to feel that sense of urgency because the End of the world and Judgement Day seemed to be close. Now, I am an old man in a hurry because I know I haven't very much time left. Death, simple extinction, is drawing near, and I must do what I can while I can. If you are reading this after my death, well, Hello from the past to you!

Notice, too, that because solar living and solar loving are by a continuing process of uninhibited self-outing, or in the philosophers' jargon "self-exteriorization," everything in a fully-solar social world is wide open and brightly-lit. There is no room for any hiddenness, deception, duplicity or concealment. Everyone must be frank. This theme is very strong in the Bible, especially in connection with the return of the heavenly world into this world: the landlord has returned, and it is time to open the books for his inspection. Everything is to be audited. All those dark corners and cupboards must be emptied out. Everything must be brought to light and made explicit. There can be no more concealment or postponement.[34]

We of course, with our advanced information technology and our freedom of information laws, live increasingly in just such a society. We all want to come out, we all want 24/7 access, everyone has a right to everything all the time. Some commentators are horrified by this extreme explicitness, and want to protect their own privacy. They follow the French philosopher Jean Baudrillard in describing a culture in which everyone lets it all hang out all the time as being literally "obscene." But I suggest that today's all-out culture is simply the long-term result of the systematic and thoroughgoing application of critical thinking to every area of cultural life. Critical thinking demands openness, *accountability*, everywhere, in a way that threatens to end the bourgeois kind of culture in which people have the right to keep the truth about themselves permanently hidden. They were—perhaps they still are—extremely secretive about their real selves, their relation to God, their politics, and most of all, their gross taxable incomes. Such a culture is a platonic sort of culture, which makes a sharp distinction between outer appearance and inner reality, and demands the right to keep up outward appearances and to keep the real truth hidden. But the development in recent centuries of critical thinking requires *everything* that has been kept hidden to be brought out into the open for public scrutiny, exactly as in the thought-world of the Bible the arrival of God in Judgement creates a demand that everyone and everything shall fully come out for inspection. Hence my argument, in this present chapter and over many years past, that our present cultural situation (post-modern, media-led, ultra-open and ultra-communicative) is *ethically and religiously* analogous to the cultural situation in which Jesus preached in Galilee. Criticism is Greek for judgment, and our critical thinking is a late recycling, after two millennia, of the ancient idea of God's coming in judgement. Both demand accountability, openness, "outing." Both demand an end to the appearance/reality distinction, *especially in ethics and religion.* All out, *now!*, they say.

Maybe we find the demand at first repugnant, and then terrifying. But we can't hide from it. In the old culture, you couldn't hide from God, for he always caught up with you. In the culture of yesterday, you couldn't hide from Death: wherever you ran to in the hope of getting away from him, he'd be there, waiting for you and saying: "Ah! we have an appointment, have we not?" And today you cannot hide from the culture of instant access to everything all the time. It'll catch up with you, and you will be exposed.

Until yesterday people believed that you could escape exposure and contingency and Death by keeping a little bit of yourself, your soul, the real You, hidden away within your heart rather as some people now have a small strongroom or bunker hidden away inside their homes to which they can retreat in an emergency. It was believed that when you withdrew into this inner citadel you could communicate directly with a God who was altogether outside space and time. In this way you could seek and find perfect security.

I am suggesting, however, that at the end of the world the Earth/Heaven distinction, the appearance/reality distinction, the public/private distinction, and indeed *all* such distinctions disappear. There is only the Now of an absolute moral choice: I must commit myself wholly to life now, I must come out without reserve, I must stop comparing myself with other people, I must completely give up *ressentiment*, and I must simply embrace and live my own contingent life wholeheartedly while I have it. To make that choice and to commit oneself to that life is the Summum Bonum, the top, the best there is for a human being. Jesus taught it in Galilee. He just happened to be the first to get the idea.[35] Others have made the same discovery, a few of them independently.[36] But nobody planned it. It was a contingent discovery, and no more. My own suggestion is that since the 1960s we have lived in an age when the message is beginning to make sense again, not just to a rare individual, but to the many.

14

DEPRECATIONS

There are various complaints and potential misunderstandings of this book that I foresee and must attempt to ward off.

A NEW GRAND NARRATIVE?

When I began the study of theology the last generation of great theologians were still alive: Barth and Bultmann in Europe, Tillich and Neibuhr in America, and a few lesser figures. Today, there are no such figures, and serious constructive theology ("dogmatic" or "systematic" theology) is scarcely being written at all, or even attempted. In the theology faculties at the universities various historical studies are pursued—biblical studies, church history, history of doctrine, religious studies—and it is still possible to write books *about* theology. Many do. But substantial works *of* theology are lacking. The subject, it seems, has died. No Pope, Archbishop or Professor produces or can produce an intellectually-serious and up-to-date defence of something that could pass for being within the limits of traditional Christian belief. The field has been abandoned to neo-conservative irrationalism.

Why? The conventional answer is that in the great traditions of German philosophy and biblical scholarship the Christian philosophy of God died in the work of Kant,

Fichte, Hegel and Schopenhauer, and then the Christian doctrine of Revelation died in the work of biblical scholars from (say) Eichhorn to D. F. Strauss. The double crisis, in philosophy and in biblical criticism, lasted from about 1780 to 1840. There were then various attempts at a counter-revolution with the help of idealist philosophy, or existentialist philosophy, or scriptural positivism; but the last of such attempts clearly ran out of steam in the 1960s. By 1970 it was all over.[37]

I now see that that answer is not quite correct. It would be better to point out that in the interesting and violent intellectual upheaval of the 1960s certain *other* Grand Narratives also died. They were, in particular, Marxism, and also the liberal belief in progress and human perfectibility to which Senator Ed Muskie appealed in his farewell speech when he dropped out of the race for the Presidency ("I still believe in the perfectibility of man"). What had happened was that the intellectual shift of the 1960s from Marx to Nietzsche, from optimistic modernism to nihilistic postmodernism, suddenly exposed the mythological character of *all* the surviving Grand Narratives that people still looked to for encouragement. A Grand Narrative was a Big Story of Everything that reassured all those caught up in it that in the long, long run Everything was going to be All Right. Since the 1930s the biggest ideological conflict had been that between Catholics and Communists, but the planned-society Scientific Humanists were also clamouring to be heard. Now, however, at the end of the Sixties and during the following debates about postmodernism, people were beginning to admit the mythological character and the absurdity of *all* such Grand Narratives—starting with those that most noisily claimed to be modern and critical, namely Marxism and planned-society scientific humanism.[38]

At the time, many theologians were quite pleased to see their noisiest rivals and enemies being suddenly humbled. What they failed to see was that they had lost their own cover. Theology itself was also now exposed as always having a mythological Grand-Narrative character about it. In the good old days between the 1930s and the mid-1960s, the days of Graham Greene, Catholics and Communists had been engaged in a debate that was highly beneficial to both parties. By taking each other seriously they had been propping each other up! They had been more *allies* than opponents. Now, both collapsed together. By the Seventies Christianity had stopped as a serious religion in the West: the best you could say was that *to some extent* Buddhism was coming forward to replace it.

Buddhism—because Buddhism doesn't need a Grand Narrative. It can get by in a nihilistic age, because it can claim that its particular path to bliss-in-Emptiness can be verified personally by the individual who follows it. Rather similarly, I have claimed that my extremely-reduced version of Christianity can get by in a nihilistic age, because its way to joy-in-Emptiness can similarly be checked out personally by anyone who follows it. What's more, we *both* of us may be right. *Both* religions may be true, in the sense that I can allow and respect the Buddhist's account of the Summum Bonum and of the Way to it; and the Buddhist (or at least, some modern Western Buddhists) may be ready to allow and respect my account of the Summum Bonum and of the Way to it. It's true that because of my Judeo-Christian background I value the body, the emotions, and sexual love, and see them all as part of the Way, whereas the traditional Buddhist will see them all as causes of suffering. But we may be able to come to terms. In which case, we may be able to regard both religions as true, and they will be related to each other very much as the Active and Contemplative Ways were related to each other in traditional Christianity. It is also possible that some Jews may be willing to join me, because I have dropped the whole of supernatural christology including even belief in Jesus' messiahship, and the title "Christ." In a fully-secular age, all that goes. Instead, I really do want to take Jesus' teaching more seriously than "Christianity" ever dreamt of taking it, and at least some "enlightened" Jews may perhaps agree with me.

However, what I surely *cannot* do is reintroduce *any* kind of Grand Narrative. After Nietzsche, we surely cannot go back to any kind of historicist optimism about the way the Whole Story of Everything is going.

In reply, I say Yes, but I still want to tell a story about the history of religions that will help us to understand why religion was always of such enormous importance to us, and did actually make us what we now are. Indeed, against a Darwinian background, one does need a theory of how it was possible for us to have come so far in such a short time, and to have become what we now are. In effect, I am saying that in order to become ourselves we *had* to go by the religious route, that is, via the heterological kind of thinking. God and spirits were *bonnes à penser*; they helped us to think, they lured us forward, and they developed us very fast. My new Grand Narrative thus invokes religion to explain how cultural evolution has been able to happen so very much more rapidly than the biological evolution that (in our scientific theory) preceded it. Religion is our mother, our old nurse, and we should love and respect it for what it has done for us. Indeed, we owe everything to it, and are still its products. As late as the eighteenth century it was still possible for people to suppose that the very first human beings could have looked around them and gone straight into natural philosophy and the causal argument for God. Today, that supposition is clearly ridiculous. My new Grand Narrative aims to offer a better story of how we got to where we are now.

The reader will have noticed that because of my thoroughgoing linguistic-idealist philosophy I have tried to write my own story of everything in the form of a history of consciousness, in words, and imagined from within. Many anthropologists, and many historians, will say that this is highly heretical, and a bad mistake. I should not have done it. Nobody nowadays dares to write books with titles like *The Savage Mind*, or *Primitive Thought*. In reply, I point out that a recapitulation of the history of consciousness is already given to us as part of our culture—for example in the Old Testament, and in children's literature. In addition, I have taken advantage of the recent revival amongst archaeologists of interest in reconstructing the thought of earlier periods. Besides, I am so old and I have been so heretical for so long that I am past caring about accusations of intellectual unsoundness.

THE END OF CHRISTOLOGY?

In the first millennium of Church history, was it the incarnation of God in Christ, or was it the death of Jesus on the Cross, that was decisive in bringing about the salvation of human beings? Often in the first millennium the answer seems to be: "The former." The incarnation was seen as having bridged the ontological gap between God and the finite mortal human being: "He became what we are, so that we might become what he is." Throughout the first millennium the whole subject of the shameful and horrific death of Jesus on the Cross was so painful that art was slow to portray it, and although it was endlessly discussed and a great many ideas were floated, no intellectually and morally satisfying way of theorizing it was ever arrived at and agreed upon. To this day there is no orthodox "doctrine of the Atonement." Certainly the first millennium found the Incarnation much easier to think than the Cross.

During the second millennium Christian metaphysics began to decline, and the culture became more individualistic. This made it seem that the barrier separating the self from God was not so much ontological as moral. In which case the Cross, and the theory of how Christ has by his death won for us the forgiveness of our sins, moves into the foreground. Christ, thought the Protestant Reformers, really did die for us and in our place. Theories of substitution followed: it seemed that God had mercifully tricked himself into being satisfied with his own Son's death in our place to placate his own wrath, or something of the kind. About such ideas, no more can or should be said.

My own view, in conclusion, is that we now have to give up the whole cycle of Christological dogmas: the Immaculate Conception (of Mary in the womb of St Anne), the Virginal Conception (of Jesus in the womb of Mary), the Incarnation, the Atonement, the Resurrection, the Ascension and Heavenly Session, the Second Coming and the Last Judgement. None of these doctrines is now rationally defensible—except that my Great Story looks for a Second Advent of the *teaching*, and not the person, of Jesus; and the Heavenly Session of Jesus may be taken as prefiguring the "anthropomonism" of more recent times. The cosmic Christ, like the cosmic Buddha, foreshadows modern radical humanism.

Unfortunately, that is not all: I have reluctantly concluded that the title "Christ" must also be given up, because it presupposes the acceptance of a theology of history in general, and Jewish national messianism in particular; and when I give up the title Christ, I have a consequent problem with words like Christian and Christianity. For me, everything is contingent, and it is just a contingent fact that a certain man named Jesus of Nazareth happened to work out for himself and to teach a way of living that seems to me to be the *Summum Bonum*, the top, the best there is for us mortal human beings. So I wish to abandon Christology altogether, and instead to focus attention upon the teaching of Jesus.

There are some further problems: the teaching of Jesus has reached us in only a very garbled form, and has not been well understood or interpreted during the past two millennia. My own reconstruction of it—or rather, of the strand in it which seems to me to be of the very highest value—is admittedly controversial. That cannot be helped: but the new Grand Narrative that I have described suggests that Jesus the teacher may yet have a future, after the end of the Church.

TOO THIN?

Historic Western Christianity was above else a Grand Narrative, a great cosmic story of Creation, Fall and Redemption big enough to give any community, however large, a sense of its place in the whole scheme of things, and of its task. The story is mythological, and cannot be told today—not even in a very reduced form. Some people have essayed a version linked with liberal belief in the progressive education of the human race, and a few have tried to make biological evolution into a new Grand Narrative. Unconvinced by them, I have built my own little story around the history of religion, and the awe and respect that most human beings (even those who most cordially dislike Christianity) still feel for the purest and most exalted strand in the tradition of Jesus' teaching. In my scheme Jesus' preaching in Galilee is *both* the highest point reached in the history of religions *and* the Fall, in that the tradition of his teaching quickly became garbled and was set aside in favour of the development of a new mediated religion focussed upon his *person*. But though Jesus' message was befogged, it was never wholly lost, and the worldwide acceptance of the moral authority of "humanitarian ethics" in the past generation or so is a clear sign that the world is more ready to hear the Galilean message today than it has ever been. Events like the reconciliation of Ian Paisley and Gerry Adams in Northern Ireland, the democratization of South Africa twenty years ago without bloodshed, and the recent international response to the Haiti earthquake, simply did not happen anywhere before the mid-twentieth

century. To compare "the condition of the working class" in
the modern West European welfare state with the condition
of the same people's forebears a century or two ago, is to see
how far we have come in just a few generations.[39]

It will be said that I haven't saved enough, and that
my account is too reductionist. But this present essay has
a limited purpose: it is asking what kind of replacement
might be available to us for the old Augustinian Grand
Narrative. In a lecture given in Cambridge in the Lent Term
of 1963, J. S. Bezzant, Dean of St John's College, told the
Augustinian story and then said that recent cultural change
and advances in knowledge had exploded the old story so
completely that "the bare recital of it has the aspect of a
malicious travesty."[40]

He was right: I was there, I recall. Here I have offered
the outline of a replacement. But I haven't by any means
attempted to give a *complete* account of the various forms
of religious life and experience that are still available to us,
even in these secular and sceptical times. That I have done
elsewhere.[41] Here, the interest is in setting out a single line
of narrative that may help us to get our bearings, and situ-
ate ourselves historically.

OVER-REACHING

A good deal of contemporary thinking has for decades been
insisting that human existence, and therefore also human
thought, are always *situated* in a particular historical and
cultural context, with the corollary that our ability to enter
imaginatively into the thinking of human beings who lived
long ago, or in culturally-remote parts of the world, is very
limited. For example, ordinary readers in the modern West
may enjoy reading novels set as far back as Jane Austen,
and a very capable biographer such as Claire Tomalin
with the help of unusually abundant evidence may be able
to convince us that we understand Samuel Pepys in the

1660s. But it is very difficult to go much (or any) further back than that. In theology, Albert Schweitzer at the very beginning of the twentieth century was ready to make bold psychological judgements about Jesus, but a generation later theologians began to insist upon the absurdity of attributing something like a modern personality to Jesus. In his case, with the further handicap of badly-contaminated evidence, the past really *is* another country. By the late twentieth century, anthropologists were beginning to have similar doubts about their own attempts to enter into the minds of preliterate, "face-to-face" peoples by the methods of "participant observation."

In the past I have generally shared these doubts, but in this essay I have rowed in the (very unfashionable) opposite direction. There are various reasons for this shift of emphasis.

One is that thinking about time and about our contemporary debates over "presentism" has led me to experiment with the view that the past is not wholly non-existent, because present reality—and, in particular, our present ways of *thinking* and our present *language*—is the accumulated legacy of the past, and includes many instructive relics of earlier states of consciousness. Dreams, panic attacks, jactations, psychological quirks, ancient linguistic usages and many other phenomena may supply ancient materials for us to excavate.

Secondly, as I have said above, we have a very strong urge to recapitulate the history of thought in the way we bring up our children and in the stories we read to them. Our religion itself is to a surprising degree just such a recapitulation. Perhaps it is more historical than it knows it is.

Thirdly, I became fascinated even as a boy with systems of thought as other worlds that we can enter into and explore. At school, Platonism and orthodox neo-darwinism (c. 1950), were examples of such thought-worlds, one of them being very "top-down" and the other very "bottom-up." Later, I found the same excitement in entering into the thought-worlds of the early-modern philosophers from Descartes to Kierkegaard. I learnt that we *can* do it, with great profit.

Fourthly, and finally, there has just been in *physical* anthropology and archaeology a half-century of rapid growth of knowledge and of reflection upon human origins. As indicated in the text, I have been interested in these developments and have been encouraged by them to think again about human beginnings, and especially about the beginnings of consciousness and knowledge.

There has been a philosophical motive for this interest. In the present essay I have repeatedly asked the reader to shut her or his eyes and go back into a time when there is nothing but obscure awareness of a heaving, speckled chaos of tiny specks against a background of darkness. I have been suggesting that by this very simple thought-experiment every single one of us can go back into the Primal Chaos, the original darkness, from which so many creation myths begin. It is instantly accessible to every one of us. That is where each of us began individually, and that is where we all began collectively. From nowhere else but in that chaotic darkness, and without any external help whatever, we humans have had to build up everything—the whole enormous complexity of modern global culture and modern knowledge. Everything is a communal human construct, built up by us without any help, and *from within* our own point of view, at first only slowly, but at a steadily accelerating pace which has been rapid for the past 5,000 years and explosive for the past 500. How *did* we do it: how did we even get started?

Religion all along gave the right answer: In the beginning was the Word, the general term, the name of the kind, a word like *Bear!*, or *Tiger!*, or *Snake!* shouted athwart the chaos. It illuminated and ordered the chaos and told us what to do: *Bolt!* It was yelled at us by the first intellectual, the sentinel lookout who vigilantly scanned the environment while we were feeding or whatever. General words such as these move across the field of consciousness, between the mind and the world. The general word was at first, and most often, the name of an animal kind, the sort of thing that nowadays we call a totem or a mascot, not any particular wolf or gazelle, but *the Wolf*, *the Gazelle*: the *kind*, and not the individual.

At some point in human evolution we gave up simple, automatic stimulus-and-reflex-response interaction with our environment, and replaced it with the sign, the word. The sign, floating between the mind and the world across the screen of consciousness, helps us to pick out something as being a gazelle or a snake. Yelled aloud, the sign communicates, binding the group together and prompting common action. In religion, the sign is regarded as a totem animal, as an ancestral animal spirit, and ultimately as an animal-headed divinity. In philosophy, the sign correspondingly evolves into the platonic idea or form, or even, sometimes, into an angel, or into an Idea in the mind of God. Alternatively, in the Aristotle-to-Wittgenstein lineage, the sign becomes a concept, and then finally just a word.

The implication of all this is that the supernatural world of religion is the "transcendental" realm, tucked away between the mind and the world, in which language moves and makes order out of the chaos of experience. And from this starting-point I have tried to suggest why and how religious thought was so overwhelmingly important to us for so long. In the long run, religion finishes its job by completely delivering the world to us as our world, and by delivering us to ourselves. Its final gift is the way of living that I have called "solar." Just to live like that *is* the Highest Good, the best there is for us.

NOTES

1. Augustine, *City of God*.
2. Hume, *Treatise of Human Nature*.
3. *Psalm* 50:10.
4. Lévi-Strauss, *Totemism*.
5. The ideas I present here are taken further in an interesting way by Maurice Bloch, *Prey into Hunter*. The Universal, the Totem animal, is immortal, so that if I can through sacrifice or in some such way identify myself with it, I may be able to gain something of its immortality for myself.
6. Referring here to Freud's *Totem and Taboo*.
7. For the role of religion in early state societies, I was much influenced, years ago, by H. Frankfort et al., *The Intellectual Adventure of Ancient Man*. The essay on the Egyptian state is particularly memorable. In the years that followed, one picked up J. B. Pritchard's monumental anthology of *Ancient Near-Eastern Texts*, and Thorkild Jacobsen, *The Treasures of Darkness*. These books remain very valuable, but the more recent works of Steven Mithen, and of David Lewis-Williams and David Pearse are based upon a much wider range of modern research, and have forced a good deal of rethinking upon me. In particular, the full-blown religious ideology of the State developed in many more places, and much more slowly, than I used to think. But it *did* develop, and it was strikingly similar in many parts of the world. Its last relics are still around.
8. D. W. Winnicott, *Playing and Reality*.
9. Evans-Pritchard himself is one of the many anthropologists who have ruminated upon the turbulent modern history of their own subject: see his *Theories of Primitive Religion*; and for another distinguished anthropologist's reflections in turn upon *him*, see Mary Douglas, *Evans-Pritchard*.
10. See Maurice Bloch's, *Prey into Hunter*.

11. E.g. Pritchard, n. 7, pp. 455ff., 611ff.
12. Jeremiah 31:31–34; Ezekiel 36:22–28, 37:1–14; Joel 2:28f., etc.
13. For the arguments in this chapter, see my *Jesus and Philosophy*.
14. That God preserves the Church from doctrinal error is *itself* part of the Church's doctrine. Derrida once wrote a whole book about the signing of the Constitution of the United States, pointing out that the signatories did not have the authority to sign the document until it had been signed. The circularity is common to all great founding documents—including infallible scriptures.
15. The figures of a cosmic man of giant size, and of the cosmos itself as shaped like a giant, are common in Asian religion. Even Islam knows of a "Perfect Man." These mythological themes testify to the ultimately-humanist orientation of religious thought everywhere. See my *The Nature of Man*, chap. 2.
16. Matthew 5:17–19.
17. *Critique of Pure Reason*, A808=B836.
18. E.g., *Tractatus*, 6.5–6.521; *Philosophical Investigations* §§ 123–29.
19. The term "Christianity" could be used in later mediaeval times to mean "piety," or a particular spirituality. The use of the term to designate a particular "religion" is associated with the Enlightenment, when each major faith tradition began to be named in that way—as "a creed." See Wilfred Cantwell Smith, *The Meaning and End of Religion*, pp. 73–79.
20. Picasso rather well illustrates Nietzsche's idea here, because he is clearly both a traditional Mediterranean—even *Homeric*—man and also a firm modernist. He seems to jump over the centuries in between.
21. Thomas L. Thompson, *The Bible in History*.
22. On this point, the writers who have attracted most attention have been the Americans Jack Miles and Harold Bloom.
23. The writer who started me thinking about the *Genesis* creation-narrative in this way was Eve Tavor Bannett. See her *Structuralism and the Logic of Dissent*.
24. The *transcendent* is a realm that lies beyond all possible experience, whereas the *transcendental* realm lies tucked away on the *near* side of experience. It comprises all the conditions of the possibility of objective experience, as worked out by Kant.
25. The grandest monument created by British rule in India was the Viceroy's Palace at Delhi, designed by Lutyens and completed just as the Raj was coming to its end.

26. In his trilogy of science-fiction novels. Lewis also wrote an excellent book about the mediaeval cosmology: *The Discarded Image*.

27. R. S. Thomas and Geoffrey Hill.

28. On the Cambridge to London railway line, one is going *up* in both directions, for one goes up to Cambridge and up to London, both places being centres.

29. Jacques Derrida's work during the 1960s is the most powerful critique of the myth of a founding Centre, or (as some say) "normative Origin."

30. The USA is in some respects exceptional, and it is hard to say why.

31. Women in particular often complain that the Latin Christian idea of the soul, which sharply divides the human self from its own body and its own emotions, is for them highly alienating. The complaint is surely justified.

32. I presented this account of selfhood in various writings of the late '80s and early '90s, including *After All*, 1994.

33. The text in which I worked out this theme best was *Solar Ethics*, 1995.

34. These themes really are very strong in the synoptic gospels, and in some other parable-tellers of Jesus' time.

35. The allusion here is to the Buddhist doctrine that there is no reason why the Buddhist way to happiness should not have been discovered accidentally from time to time by other seekers after salvation who did not have the benefit of receiving the truth from a Teacher of good lineage. Similarly, I give up the traditional idea of the uniqueness and sole sufficiency of Christ on the grounds that for all I know other people may have quite independently discovered Jesus' way to happiness by solar living and loving. Since the way is verifiable by anyone who chooses to follow it, its value does not depend upon any claims about its precise historical origin.

36. For a fuller account of Jesus, see my *Jesus and Philosophy*.

37. See Hugh McLeod, *The Religious Crisis of the 1960s*, and the works of Callum G. Brown.

38. J.-F. Lyotard, *The Postmodern Condition*, was influential in showing that "scepticism towards Grand Narratives" is a leading characteristic of postmodern thinking.

39. See my *The Meaning of the West*.

40. See D. M. McKinnon and others, *Objections to Christian Belief*.

41. Most recently, in *Theology's Strange Return*.

BOOKS REFERRED TO

I list here the modern (and some older) books referred to in the main text and the notes, specifying the editions from which I have quoted. Most are UK editions: where an independent US edition exists, I cite it, too.

Augustine. *Concerning the City of God against the Pagans.* Trans. Henry Bettenson. Intro. David Knowles. Harmondsworth, Middx and Baltimore, Maryland: Penguin Books, 1972.

Eve Tavor Bannett. *Structuralism and the Logic of Dissent.* London and New York: Macmillan, 1989.

Maurice Bloch. *Prey into Hunter: The Politics of Religious Experience.* Cambridge: Cambridge University Press, 1972.

Callum G. Brown. *The Death of Christian Britain: Understanding Secularization 1800–2000.* 2nd ed. London: Routledge, 2009.

Don Cupitt. *The Nature of Man.* London: SPCK, 1979.

_____. *After All.* London: SCM Press, 1994.

_____. *Solar Ethics.* London: SCM Press, 1994.

_____. *Impossible Loves.* Santa Rosa, CA: Polebridge Press, 2007.

_____. *The Meaning of the West.* London: SCM Press, 2008.

_____. *Jesus and Philosophy.* London: SCM Press, 2009.

_____. *Theology's Strange Return.* London: SCM Press, 2010.

Richard Dawkins. *The God Delusion.* London: Black Swan, 2007.

Mary Douglas. *Evans-Pritchard.* Glasgow: Collins (Fontana Modern Masters); New York: Viking Press, 1980.

E. E. Evans-Pritchard. *Theories of Primitive Religion.* Oxford: The Clarendon Press, 1965.

H. and H. A. Frankfort, John A. Wilson, Thorkild Jacobsen and William A. Irwin. *The Intellectual Adventure of Ancient Man: An Essay on Speculative Thought in the Ancient Near East.* Chicago: The University of Chicago Press, 1946 =

Before Philosophy: The Intellectual Adventure of Ancient Man. Harmondsworth: Penguin Books, 1949.

S. Freud. *Totem and Taboo.* 1913, Eng. trans. 1918, many editions.

David Hume. *A Treatise of Human Nature.* Edited with an analytical index by L. A. Selby-Bigge. 2d ed. with text rev. and variant readings by P. H. Nidditch. Oxford: The Clarendon Press; New York: Oxford University Press, 1978.

Thorkild Jacobsen. *The Treasures of Darkness: A History of Mesopotamian Religion.* New Haven, CT: Yale University Press, 1976.

Claude Lévi-Strauss. *Totemism.* Trans. Rodney Needham. Harmondsworth: Penguin Books, 1973.

C. S. Lewis. *The Discarded Image.* Cambridge: Cambridge University Press, 1964.

David Lewis-Williams and David Pearse. *Inside the Neolithic Mind.* London: Thames and Hudson, 2009.

David Lewis-Williams. *The Mind in the Cave.* London: Thames and Hudson, 2002.

J.-F. Lyotard. *The Postmodern Condition: A Report on Knowledge.* Manchester University Press, 1984.

Hugh McLeod. *The Religious Crisis of the 1960s.* Oxford: Oxford University Press, 2007, 2010.

D. M. McKinnon and others. *Objections to Christian Belief.* London: Constable, 1963; Penguin Books 1965.

Steven Mithen. *The Prehistory of the Mind.* London: Phoenix/Orion, 1998.

————. *After the Ice.* London: Phoenix/Orion, 2004.

J.B. Pritchard, ed. *Ancient Near-Eastern Texts relating to the Old Testament.* 3rd ed. Princeton, NJ: Princeton University Press, 1969.

Colin Renfrew and Ezra B.W. Zubrow. *The Ancient Mind: Elements of Cognitive Archaeology.* Cambridge: Cambridge University Press, 1994.

Wilfred Cantwell Smith. *The Meaning and End of Religion.* New York: Macmillan, 1962; London: SPCK, 1978.

Thomas L. Thompson. *The Bible in History: How Writers Create a Past.* London: Jonathan Cape, 1999

Edward Burnett Tylor. *Primitive Culture.* 2 vols. London: Murray, 1871.

D. W. Winnicott. *Playing and Reality.* London: Tavistock Publications; New York: Basic Books, 1971.

INDEX

Breinigsville, PA USA
13 December 2010
251269BV00004B/2/P